Tawanda Prince

Thunder Knocking at My Heart
Living through the Storm of a Life Shattered

From the Heart!

[signature] 2016

Thunder Knocking at My Heart
Living through the Storm of a Life Shattered

Tawanda Prince

Tawanda Prince

Copyright © 2016 Tawanda Prince

Printed and bound in the United States of America. All rights reserved. No part of this book may be reproduced or transmitted in any form or by any means, electronic or mechanical, including photocopying, recording, or by an information storage or retrieval system, except by a reviewer who may quote brief passages in a review to be printed in a magazine or newspaper, without permission in writing form the publisher.
This book is an account of a true story. I have tried to recreate events, locales and conversations from my memories of them. In order to maintain their anonymity and protect the privacy of individuals, in some instances I have changed the names of individuals and places, and I may have changed some identifying characteristics and details such as physical properties, occupations and places of business.

Scripture quotations marked (NKJ) are taken from New King James Version®. Copyright © 1982 by Thomas Nelson, Inc. Used by permission. All rights reserved.
Scripture quotations marked (NIV) are taken from the Holy Bible, New International Version®, NIV®. Copyright © 1973, 1978, 1984, 2011 by Biblica, Inc.™ Used by permission of Zondervan. All rights reserved worldwide. www.zondervan.com The "NIV" and "New International Version" are trademarks registered in the United States Patent and Trademark Office by Biblica, Inc.™
Scripture quotations marked KJV are from the King James Version.

Printed in the United States of America
20 19 18 17 16   987654321

Published by Rosie Lane Publishing *Rosielanepublishing@comcast.net*
Author's website: *www.Thegoodlifecoach.net*
Tawandaprince@comcast.net

ISBN: 978-0-692-63208-6
Book design: Tawanda Prince
Cover design: Kendall King- *kkproductions.biz*
Back cover photograph: Portrait Artist Jackie Hicks
Editor: Jacinda Smith White aka Hope J. Springs

DEDICATION

This book is dedicated to those who are living with or have survived a "broken" heart.

"Create in me a clean heart and renew a right spirit within me." Psalm 51:10 KJV

Tawanda Prince

Thunder Knocking at my Heart

ACKNOWLEDGEMENTS

First, I give God all the glory for the great, wondrous and mighty things he has done. Miracles still happen and God still brings forth life from that which was dead. I praise the name of Jesus.

I would like to acknowledge all those who have journeyed with me through the storm. To anyone who helped to hold up the umbrella when the rain came down and/or picked up the pieces after the storm.

To my parents who have gone above and beyond to support my vision, dreams and mission. Thanks for being the wind beneath my wings…in and out of the storm.

To the investment firm of A & R, thank you for sowing many seeds and may you reap a bountiful harvest. How much do I owe you again?

To my children: I am so blessed and grateful that God has allowed me to watch you grow. You both are my inspiration, motivation and drive. I have to keep writing books so I can keep buying more rotisserie chickens. Thanks for believing in me.

To my "creativity circle": I am grateful for the creative energy and encouragement that you all continuously pour into me, while yet creating your own masterpieces. Journey thanks for "find and replace." Truly, birds of a feather, pontificate together.

To my editor, Jacinda Smith White aka Hope J. Springs, thank you for your obedience to the voice of God. Your skills, gifts, talents and spirit were the missing pieces to the puzzle. You were there when "THUNDER" knocked and I'm so glad that we are together again. Thanks for your help…especially since I needed it completed YESTERDAY!

Tawanda Prince

     Miss Essie, thank you for the title of my book and for caring for my "broken" heart. I will be eternally grateful for your love and support.

     To the medical team who has cared for me over the years, thank you for caring hands that mend hearts and lives. For it takes many bricks to build a strong tower.

     To the readers; thanks for your support. May your lives be enriched by my story and may you be victorious when facing a storm.

Table of Contents

1. The Forecast — 9
2. Fixin' for a Twister — 12
3. The Road Not Taken — 20
4. It's Gonna Rain — 25
5. Deep Waters — 31
6. A 23-hour tour — 36
7. I See You — 40
8. Scattered Clouds, Chance of Showers — 49
9. A Table for One — 54
10. The Heart of the Matter — 61
11. Knock, Knock Who's There — 68
12. The Storm is Passing Over — 73
13. The Awakening — 78
14. The Eye of the Storm — 83
15. There is Power in the Blood — 97
16. Family Reunion — 105
17. Homeward Bound — 111
18. A Table for Two — 117
19. After the Storm — 127
20. Yet Still I Rise — 134
21. The Test of the Storm — 138
22. Author's Note — 153

Tawanda Prince

The Forecast

He draws up the drops of water which distill as rain to the streams; the clouds pour down their moisture and abundant showers fall on the human race. Who can understand how He spreads out the clouds, how He thunders from His pavilion? See how He scatters His lightning about Him, bathing the depths of the sea. This is the way He governs the nations and provides food in abundance. He fills His hands with lightning and commands it to strike its mark. His thunder announces the coming storm. Job 36: 27-33 NIV

I awakened from a sleep like no other, eyes heavy and body unfamiliar. I saw, yet I didn't see; I heard, yet I didn't hear. I believed, yet I didn't believe. *White.* All I saw was *white.* All I smelled was *white.* All I tasted was *white.* I thought to myself, as I transitioned from *white* to black,

"This white over my head is not a cloud, and it's not a coffin, I must be alive." It was my awakening.

I awakened from a new sleep and yet an old sleep. A sleep with promise, a sleep of transformation. A journey ending and a journey beginning. The passing into a season of change. As I came into awareness of my condition, I recognized that nothing was as it had been, and it would not be the same again.

My body ached and my heart was broken. I cried and I screamed yet unable to make a sound with the tube in my throat. I was afraid, very afraid. Afraid of seeing death and afraid of facing life shattered. It was an awakening like no other.

Perhaps, the recovery room should be aptly renamed the "awakening room." For it was the place where I awakened to face the wreckage that remained after my storm had ended. It was the place where I began to gather the fragments of a broken body and shattered life. It was the place where I awakened to face my uncertain future. It was where I discovered the

Tawanda Prince

difference between waking up and awakening. I had an awakening!

Chapter 2

Fixin' for a Twister

I will uphold you with My righteous right hand. Isaiah 41:10 NIV

January 11, 1999 was no ordinary Monday. It was the Monday that I was to return to work after more than two months of maternity leave. Sadie was just a few days short of two months, and I faced the separation anxiety that every working mother of a newborn probably faces. J.C. was just a little over two years old, and I was up to my elbows in bottles, diapers, baby poop and toddler mess.

I agonized over the fact that I would have to leave them while I went to work. They were my babies, and at 37 years old, I wasn't planning to have any more children. However, I agonized even more over the arduous task of managing a household, husband, two children and completing the final semester of my

Master's degree program. Although I was accustomed to wearing that **"S"** on my chest and leaping from tall buildings in a single bound, I was growing weary. Recently, sleep had become unfamiliar to me and my "IQ" (irritability quotient) was falling by the minute. I was losing myself in my superwoman fantasy and for the record I wasn't even having fun.

So just how does a superwoman arrange all of the hats that she wears? I was the maid, the cook, the nanny, the chauffer, the teacher, the student, his mistress and yet, his wife. Oh yes, I had bought into the superwoman myth, and I was expected to balance everything and wear a smile, while bowing and scraping and making sure everyone's needs were met, leaving mine neglected. I was rapidly spiraling downward to a place from which I was unsure I could return. Inside I was screaming and kicking, but I had no time for a breakdown because I had to return to work.

My situation brings to mind the Broadway musical stage play, The Wiz, which is a story of overcoming obstacles when the winds of adversity blow in your life. Ironically, I had an opportunity to perform in this play in a local college production just a few years prior. In the beginning of the story, the character of Uncle Henry warns, "We're fixin' for a twister." The storm that came whisked Dorothy, the main character, off to worlds unknown. Along her journey, Dorothy met up with a few characters and situations that represented not only her personal struggles but also many of life's inner obstacles that hold one back from fulfilling one's destiny and purpose. In the process, she discovers that the strength, courage and wisdom that she needed were deep down inside all along. She finally sees the light and finds her way "home." In order to reach that special place, Dorothy had to come through the storm.

  So there I was, like Dorothy, in the Wiz, *fixin' for a twister*. Somewhere off in the distance the storm was headed my way. I could smell the changes in the air. If I listened carefully, I could hear the thunder rolling in the distance. I could even see flashes of lightning ready to destroy anything in its path. A twister that would stir up and crash down anything that was left unprotected. What I didn't know was even though I had no jacket, no umbrella and no hat, I was covered by God's almighty wings.

    Despite the fact that I was *fixin' for a twister*, I returned to work on Monday, January 11, 1999. I worked at Southern Maryland High School, in Southern, Maryland, with 70 miles round trip for travel. This, combined with three daycare transactions per day, was enough to wear me down. My husband helped with dropping off J.C. in the morning to a neighborhood daycare center, but I was responsible for dropping off Sadie and picking up both of them in the evening. My work day began early with a sign-in time of 7:20 a.m., which made my morning very hectic to say the least.

    On top of all of the other drama, there was the actual job. I was an English teacher who was loved by my students but perhaps not so much by the administration. In fact, my professional style and personality was irritating and challenging to a few key players of the Southern Maryland High School family. In other words, one or two people in key positions, who were not a part of the Tawanda Prince Fan Club, were not happy that I was returning. Consequently these same individuals saw to it that my transition from home base to "homeroom" was not easy.

While on maternity leave, my classes had been temporarily reassigned. However, upon my return I was informed that the teacher who had taken the classes in my absence would continue for the remainder of the fall semester, which was about another two weeks. This meant that I would have to float to help out wherever I was needed, and teach at least one of the classes that I had previously. Additionally, I was scheduled for a professional observation by an Administrator on my first Friday back to work. Yes, I was *fixin' for a twister*, nonetheless, I went to work. The first day seemed endless, and I longed to hold my newborn baby in my arms. I just wanted to kiss her, smell her sweetness, feel her softness and believe that all was right with the world.

On Tuesday, January 12, 1999, the staff had a meeting. Just as Moses beat his "staff" upon the rock and blood came pouring out, our "staff" meeting was the same way. It seemed that we too had been beaten upon a rock, by our leaders, until blood spilled out. During the meeting, our principal chastised and challenged us to give just a little more than the 150% that most of us were already giving. From his point of view, it wasn't right until it was 10 degrees beyond perfect. At the conclusion of the meeting, I ran over to my friend and confidant, Jen, and cried out, "I can't do this anymore, and I just can't take it!" As Jen reminded me of my strength in Christ, it was painfully clear that I was *fixin' for a twister.*

After the staff meeting, I made my second attempt to leap tall buildings in a single bound, and complete my evening daycare run. That day had been my second attempt to climb "Mount Impossible." I had made it through the morning routine and faced the day with courage. I was not happy about being there but I made it through with all of the fortitude of a soldier. However, the evening had its own set of challenges. Sadie and JC were in 2 separate daycares, about 20 miles apart. Neither place accepted children from both age groups. Therefore, Sadie was at an in home day care provider, in Glenarden, Maryland. J.C. attended Early Learning Development Center, in Laurel, Maryland, near our house. Coordinating the drop off and pick up logistics seemingly required the skills of an air traffic controller.

    I arrived late to pick up J.C. Sadie was neatly tucked away in her carrier in the back seat and I had mashed the gas to the floor to be on time. Frantically I tore through the door to face the waiting care providers who were ready to go home. The director could tell by the harried and frustrated look on my face that I was having a tough time. I asked her to step outside with me while I helped J.C. to get in the car. The tears that had welded up behind my eyelids threatened to burst forward. With the weight of my world on my shoulders, I wept as I told her about my challenges. Expressing compassion, she assured me that everything would somehow workout.

    That night, I knew for sure that I *was fixin' for a twister*. The clouds formed overhead and darkness lurked in the shadows and the rushing winds of change were blowing in my life from all directions. Shutters flapped, trees swayed, dust blew and the storm was imminent.

Chapter 3

The Road Not Taken

"...Yet knowing how way leads on to way,
I doubted if I should ever come back.
I shall be telling this with a sigh
Somewhere ages and ages hence:
Two roads diverged in a wood, and I-
I took the one less traveled by,
And that has made all the difference."
Robert Frost

Thursday, January 14, 1999 was my parents 38th wedding anniversary. Truly, it was a day of celebration for our family which turned out to be a sad day for me. I was unaware that the road I was traveling on would require bigger boots than I was wearing.

Tawanda Prince

Typical of January, the weather was awful that day and snow and ice storms rocked most of the eastern seaboard. I went to work praying that we would be released early from school due to inclement weather. The county school system often waited until the last minute to make schedule adjustments based on the weather.

Since my schedule was still erratic from maternity leave, it would be another hectic day of moving from pillar to post. However, I needed to put the final touches on my lesson plan because I was going to be observed by an administrator on the next day.

I had decided to wrap up the final unit of study on poetry with a special project. I was going to have the students work on this project during my observation.

The project was called, "In the Bag," which involved using a small, brown, paper bag. The students would select a poem that they liked and understood. Using magazines, they would cut out pictures of symbols represented in the poem. So if the poem was written about trees and flowers, the student would cut out pictures of trees and flowers. These pictures or symbols would then be glued to the outside of the bag. They could also use their creativity to enhance the bag with additional decorations.

    The second portion of the project involved using items that represented the symbols in the poem. Likewise artificial plants or flowers might represent a poem about trees and flowers. These items would then be placed inside the bag. Each student would read their poem and then present their "bag" to the class.

    I was excited about this project because it would be my first time using it. I had gotten the idea from a colleague, Roberta Olstein, and I had embellished it to fit my style and lesson objectives. I loved this project because it gave the students a chance to express their ideas in creative and exciting ways. It also gave me a chance to identify their strengths and weaknesses, evaluate their progress and have poetry fun with my students. I just knew that the administrator would not only be impressed with me, but also with my students. I was proud to show that I could bounce back and thrive amidst all of the chaos. I was eager to prove that I was a good teacher and that you can't keep a good teacher down. So, armed with my spectacular project, on Thursday, January 14, 1999, I prepared for my observation.

As was customary, I created a sample "poetry bag" to model the lesson for the students. I had selected the famous poem by Robert Frost, "The Road Not Taken." I can recall reading this poem as a child in the fourth grade. Oddly enough this poem stuck in my mind since that time. I seem to share a kindred understanding of the very essence of the poem. I had committed the poem to memory for a class assignment and the most important lines of the poem have remained in my head since that time.

There was no way that I could know that as I was creating a project about "The Road Not Taken," I was standing at the cross-roads of my own life. The road that lay just ahead would be filled with hills, valleys, twists, turns, pit stops and roadblocks. I was about to face an obstacle course that would require running toward a higher calling and careful navigation of *the road not taken.*

> **Brothers and sisters, I do not consider myself yet to have taken hold of it. But one thing I do: Forgetting what is behind and straining toward what is ahead, I press on toward the goal to win the prize for which God has called me heavenward in Christ Jesus.**
> **Philippians 3:13-15 NIV**

Chapter 4

It's Gonna Rain, It's Gonna Rain!

When He thunders, the waters in the heavens roar; He makes clouds rise from the ends of the earth. He sends lightning with rain and brings out the wind from His storehouses. Jeremiah 10:13 NIV

While preparing the Poetry Bag project, I realized that all of the teachers in my section of the building had gone home. I felt a little anxious and the indigestion that started earlier while eating my lunch was really beginning to bother me. I put the project away and gathered up my things to head down the hall to the main office.

A few stragglers lingered in the office making preparations to weather the storm. The school nurse, Mrs. Miles, was calling home to check to see if her children were safely home from the ice storm. By this time, I really didn't feel well. I Nurse Miles to come into a small conference room, in the main office.

 I kept trying to burp because of the indigestion; however, I noticed that the pressure was intensifying. I just couldn't seem to get any relief no matter what I did. Nurse Miles asked me what was wrong with me. I explained that my chest and back were hurting. I refused to let her call 911, but I agreed to let her check me out. School nurses are only permitted to perform preliminary triage functions; such as, monitoring heart rate, blood pressure, body temperature, pulse and other basic body functions.

 Nurse Miles checked my heart rate with her stethoscope and everything appeared normal. By this time the indigestion was really bothering me. A few people had gathered and concern was beginning to mount. One of the office staff gave me two Rolaids to relieve the pressure in my chest. I immediately threw up the Rolaids along with my lunch. It became painfully obvious that something was seriously wrong with me.

Taking matters into her own hands, Nurse Miles ran down to her office to get her blood pressure cuff. Several coworkers tried to comfort me while she was gone. The pain and pressure were increasing as I lie on the couch in the small office. There weren't any windows in the room and the walls were beginning to close in on me. It was hot, and I began to shed the layers of clothing that I had worn to buffer that cold, icy, January day.

As she returned, my anxiety was increased. She quickly checked my blood pressure. She remembered from my pregnancy that I had extremely low blood pressure. When she checked me, my usual 90/60 reading was elevated to 160/something too high. At this point she insisted on calling 911. I did not resist because I realized that I was sick and needed medical attention.

Tawanda Prince

My breathing was shallow and labored, and I was hot. There was pain in my chest; my back hurt, and I was very uncomfortable in the small room. I clutched at my chest to try to alleviate the pain, but it didn't help. No matter where I pressed, I couldn't release the pressure that I felt. I choked and gasped a bit, as it was difficult to get air. The storm outside paralleled the storm raging in my body and my mind. I prayed for God to help me weather the storm. I saw panic on all of the faces in the room. We waited for what seemed an eternity for the EMS team to respond and since it took so long my coworkers made another 911 call.

It was at this time that I met JUMBO. Allow me to introduce you to him. JUMBO is the elephant that was sitting on my chest. He was a rude fellow, who decided that the center of my chest was where he would make himself at home. He plopped down, and snuggled in applying the full pressure of his weight on me. No matter what I did I couldn't get JUMBO to move. He became heavier by the minute and my

Thunder Knocking at my Heart

breathing became harder by the second. JUMBO was fearlessly taking over.

When the EMS team finally arrived, they assessed my condition, and I grew increasingly annoyed by the barrage of questions that I had to answer. After all, couldn't the staff tell them my name, age and other essential data? In my opinion, all they needed to know was that JUMBO was camping out on my chest and he needed to be evicted, immediately. I soon caught on that they were assessing my condition based on my responses to the questions. Finally, they loaded JUMBO and me onto the stretcher and carried us to the waiting ambulance.

Southern Medical Hospital was just a short ride from the school. However, the ice storm made navigation challenging. The EMS tech hooked me up to an oxygen tank and my breathing became a little easier. However, JUMBO was locked in position with no plans of leaving any time soon.

Tawanda Prince

Upon arrival at the Emergency Room, the ambulance doors flew open. I looked up only to see one of my former students, Arty, who was the EMS attendant. Ironically, Arty had previously responded to another emergency call when I became ill in a local store, when I was pregnant. While riding along, I didn't know that Arty was part of the team because two teams responded to the two calls that the staff had made. As I looked at him, I briefly recalled when Arty was in my tenth grade English class. He was a student who was often distracted by his obsession with becoming a fire fighter. I would often admonish him for not giving his best effort in my class. How ironic is it that Arty would be the one to respond to the call to save my life.

As they were pulling JUMBO and me off of the truck, I looked up in my former student's face and said, "Arty you are just determined to see me naked." Everybody laughed except JUMBO. He applied more pressure. I knew that I was in *deep waters*.

Chapter 5

Deep Waters

Then he got into the boat and his disciples followed him. Without warning, a furious storm came up on the lake, so that the waves swept over the boat. But Jesus was sleeping. The disciples went and woke Him, saying, 'Lord save us! We're going to drown!' He replied, 'you of little faith, why are you so afraid?' Then He got up and rebuked the winds and the waves, and it was completely calm. The men were amazed and asked, 'What kind of man is this? Even the winds and the waves obey Him! Matthew 8:23-27NIV

One always knows when surrounded by *deep waters*. The waters of change are usually colder, rougher, darker, deeper and very unpredictable to those in the boat. One is never comfortable in the waters of change but it is necessary for one to brave the rough and deep waters to get to the "other side." As they lifted me out of the ambulance, I knew that I was in the *deep waters* of change.

They wheeled me into the very familiar Emergency Room of Southern Medical Hospital. The ER staff settled me into the very unsettling ER cubicle and hooked me up to the necessary equipment. Since I was still experiencing pain from JUMBO sitting on my chest, the nurse administered the customary three doses of nitro glycerin to relieve me. This medication is usually given to patients who are experiencing severe chest pains. For some it can be a lifesaver. For me, it was the perfect solution for getting JUMBO off of my chest.

The following hours were filled with a parade of doctors, nurses, lab technicians and the like, busy about the business of taking care of me. Jen, from my job, was by my side. My husband had been notified and he was on his way through the ice storm.

The waves were quickly rising. The tide grew rougher, and it was becoming increasingly difficult for me to stay in the boat. It was a scary time. I had been in the hospital before and had come through the Emergency Room many times, but this time was different. I lay there thinking of the possibilities, wondering about my fate, fearing the worse for my future.

Then the testing began. One stick, jab, poke and prod after another. Blood tests, urine tests, x-rays, CT scans still left the medical team puzzled about my situation. Did I have a heart attack or just angina? Angina is severe chest pain brought on by a number of factors. Somewhere deep inside, I had a feeling that I was experiencing more than angina.

As I lay there stranded in the *deep waters*, I realized just how fragile this life is. Life offers no guarantees; one minute you are fine in the boat, and the next minute you are smack dab in the middle of *deep waters*...looking for a paddle. The funny thing about being in the *deep* is that God is the only one who can help because he controls the tide. No matter how deep the water, only God can keep you afloat.

From that point on, everything became surreal for me. That is, it felt like I was watching someone else's "boat" turn upside down. I knew that this time something was different. It was like I was watching a movie that involved the characters of my own life.

My husband arrived and my coworker passed on the torch. Although he was afraid and confused about exactly what was happening, he knew that our boat had hit *deep waters*. He offered as much comfort as he could, yet all the while struggling with where our boat had sailed.

It was a Thursday, and he had a scheduled performance that evening in Washington, D.C. As a jazz musician, he almost never missed a gig so he wasn't happy about this schedule interruption. The truth is that making all of the recent family adjustments challenged our marriage and this was adding another layer to the stress. Nevertheless, he was there to offer as much support as he could.

After all of the tests, analysis, diagnosis and conclusions, the final decision was that I would remain in the hospital for a 23-hour observation period. This signaled to me that they did not really know what had happened to me but they were playing it safe. We all knew that I was in *deep waters*. I was moved from the Emergency Room to a step-down unit for heart patients. Eventually, Husband left and I was alone in the boat. The waters were steadily rising and my boat was beginning to sink. At this point there was no way that I could know just what was going to happen to my boat.

Chapter 6

A Twenty-Three Hour Tour

Let not your heart be troubled, neither let it be afraid. John 14:27 KJV

When I was a child, I loved the television sitcom, *Gilligan's Island.* The show follows the escapades of seven people who started out on a three-hour boat tour that never ends. Each episode of the show involved the group trying to find their way off of the deserted island back to life as they once knew it. The group operated in survival mode, always making the best of a bad situation.

Likewise, even though I didn't know it at the time, I too was embarking on a "twenty three hour tour" that would last a lifetime. I thought it strange to be given instructions to stay in the hospital for twenty-three hours. Why twenty-three hours instead of twenty-four? Was this some insurance loophole? Was one hour really a major deciding factor? They assured me that it was for observation purposes. Little did I know just how much trouble was on the horizon.

After I settled into my new room, I ate dinner. I thought it was quite peculiar that they would serve me a pork medallion in the cardiac unit. Nevertheless I ate and tried to make the mental adjustment to where I was.

I found favor with nurse Pam, and she tried to calm my anxiety. I was concerned and afraid of what was going on. I couldn't sleep, and I couldn't get comfortable with the heart monitor around my neck. I also missed my babies very much. After all my Sadie was still in the bonding stage at two months old and I didn't like her not being with me. The unit that I was in had all of the patients hooked up to heart monitors that were manned by the nurses at the nurse's station. It was obvious to me that there was great concern for the condition of my heart.

At some time after midnight, I was talking on the phone with my mother. I couldn't seem to shake the anxiety. In the midst of our conversation, a team of medical personnel came to get me. They informed me that the blood tests taken earlier, revealed a problem and that I was being moved to the Intensive Care Unit (ICU). Immediately, my chest began to hurt.

The nurses all moved with that sense of urgency and precision that is used when a patient is in trouble. They worked at breakneck speed to gather my belongings and transfer me onto a gurney. I was hooked up to a portable heart monitor, and as the discomfort grew worse the anxiety mounted.

My heart was pounding rapidly and my chest was hurting again. I was really confused about what was going on. I questioned the nurse that I had found favor with. She responded, "Oh they haven't told you what happened? If they didn't tell you, then I can't."

Instantly I knew the deal. The nurse then began to ramble on about how unlikely and unusual it was for this to happen to someone like me. As they whisked me off to ICU, instinctively, I knew that I had had a heart attack.

    The questions and fears flooded my mind. I couldn't make sense out of everything, yet some things seemed very clear. It was clear to me that in a flash, my life was changed. It was clear that I would need to make major life adjustments to accommodate this new condition. I thank God that He only reveals to us bits and pieces of His plans for us. If I had known at that time what was ahead, I might have given up the fight.

Chapter 7

I See You!

But the eyes of the LORD are on those who fear Him, on those whose hope is in His unfailing love. Psalm 33:18 NIV

The journey to the I.C.U. seemed like a thousand miles. My chest was really hurting, and I was concerned about what was next. There were so many questions. Could I have another heart attack? Why was I moved to the I.C.U.? Where was the doctor? When could I talk to my family? What about my babies? What were they going to do to me in the I.C.U.? What was God doing with me?

I See You...

The pain intensified and my questions went unanswered. Finally the nurse gave me the magic wonder drug, morphine to relieve the pain. I couldn't help but to recall that morphine was used during the war for wounded soldiers who were experiencing extreme pain. I was indeed a wounded soldier in extreme pain. Thank God that sleep came quickly.

I See You...

The next morning I awakened even more confused than ever. I did not like the I.C.U. There was a spirit of death, not life, hovering over the unit. People whispering, watching and waiting to see who would transition from life to death. Restricted movements and careful conversations patrolled the unit. Visitations were limited to immediate family and those passing for family. Patients were cut off and disconnected from the world beyond the I.C.U.

I See You...

It is wonderful to know that no matter where I may be, God sees me there and hears my prayers. Even though I was cut off and separated from my loved ones, I was not separated from the one who loves me the most. It was a comfort to know that his love could reach me anywhere, even in the I.C.U.

For I am persuaded that neither death nor life, nor angels nor principalities nor powers, nor things present nor things to come, nor height nor depth, nor any other created thing, shall be able to separate us from God's love. Romans 8: 38 NKJV

I See You…

Under the watchful eyes of the nurses, I was not allowed to get out of the bed for anything. They continued to drug me with morphine to ease the pain and I believe to keep me contained. I was concerned about visitors because they were restricting visitation. I really needed to see my loved ones. What about my babies? I wanted my babies! They needed me and I needed them, but I was being held hostage in the I.C.U.

I See You…

As always, God had a plan that I couldn't see from where I lay. He had worked out details that I could not have even dreamed to ask for. It is impossible to see supernatural things with the natural eye.

Much to my surprise on that day I had a steady stream of visitors. It was funny that as an only child I had suddenly acquired a blood line of "sisters," who bulldozed their way pass the ICU infantry to get to me. Jen from my job came to see about me. We talked, prayed and cried together. To comfort me, she read from the book of Psalms in the Bible. She sat next to my bed, right by the window. I drifted in and out of sleep. A deep, penetrating feeling of comfort and peace surrounded me for the first time since JUMBO sat on my chest.

I See You…

My parents arrived later that day. I was excited and relieved to see them. Fear was a common thread that ran between us. Our family was in an unexpected crisis, and this was one that my parents could not fix. The feeling of helplessness was etched on each of their faces, and I pitied them just as much as they pitied me.

This was clearly a job for the Master. The same question echoed in the minds of us all. There was no question of whether God could fix it; the question was, "Would he fix it?"

I See You...

In an effort to allow maximum accessibility to me at Southern Medical Hospital, my co-worker, Jen offered to let my parents stay at her house, right near the hospital. It was comforting to know that they would be just down the road and could rush to my side when needed. My parents accepted her gracious offer, of course not knowing how long they would need to stay. They had been stuck in New York in the storm and the travel conditions and my condition were both uncertain. Just like the meteorologist indicated, we were on high alert.

I See You...

I really did not like being in the ICU. First, it was dark and gloomy. Even though there was a window in the room, it was dark. My cubicle was sectioned off by a curtain, which restricted my view but not my hearing. I could hear everything happening on the other side of the curtain. This included a code blue call for a patient in the next cubicle from me. Code blue is a signal given in the hospital when a patient stops breathing, loses blood pressure and pulse, and is declared medically dead. When the code is given, a specialized team is dispatched to attempt to restore the patient and a defibrillator is used to "shock" or jumpstart the heart to regular beating capacity. As the "blue" team rushed through the ICU unit to assist the patient, a cold chill went through me. I thought, *What if that happens to me?* The possibility of that was terribly frightening, and it disturbed me to the point of unrest.

    Additionally, the patient in the cubicle next to me was facing the possibility of death. Through the curtain, I could hear a clergyman administering the last rights to the dying patient. The family had gathered to say their possible last goodbye's as their loved one faced the possible transition from life to death. I could hear weeping and anguish as I listened through the curtain. I was frightened as I pondered again, *"What if that happens to me?"*

I See You…

I spent the rest of the day trying to find security enveloped in the love of my parents and trying to make sense of it all. There were lots of questions, yet answers were scarce. One thing was certain; I wanted off of "death row," otherwise known as ICU. I was not allowed to get out of the bed except to sit on the potty chair. Yuk!!! I hated that too, but it was a lot better than a bed pan. I was still pumped up with morphine and the high rendered me listless, and a bit disoriented. I wanted to be in the comfort of my own home holding my babies and searching for the TV remote under the couch, not in the ICU searching for the meaning of all this drama.

I See You…

By Sunday, the ICU situation was really getting to me. I was depressed and I needed relief. That afternoon, as I lay there like a bump on a log, I heard the curtain move. When I looked up, it was my best friend from 9th grade, Chanell. When she heard the news, she drove up from North Carolina to see about me. She was uncertain of the location, all she had was the hospital name. Somewhat familiar with the Maryland area, she found me. Words cannot express what that meant to me. I knew I was loved, and I needed all the love that I could get to get me through the storm. I also knew that if Chanell came all the way from North Carolina, this thing was very serious. As I tried to recover from that shock, the curtain moved all the way back, and it was my Delta Sigma Theta Sorority sister, Kenya. I was both overjoyed and overwhelmed. It is fair to say that these two were a breath of life to me. God sent them to be a dose of good medicine to heal my "broken" heart. As a nurse, Kenya paid close attention to my medical condition, care and prognosis. She was well aware of what I was facing. God always sends the right people at the right time. This in no way minimizes my appreciation for all of my other visitors, but these two were the biggest surprise.

I See You…

That Sunday evening, Dr. Abdul ordered me to return to the cardiac step down unit, with diagnostic tests pending. Wow!! I was being released from death row, or so it seemed. In my book, things were looking up. As I returned to the unit, I was able to move around and eat like I wanted to. Visitors came and went, and it was like a coming out party, but I wasn't really "out" yet. I was set to be released in two days upon completion of the diagnostic tests. I thought to myself, I will be home in two days…

I See You…

He will keep him in perfect peace whose mind is stayed on thee because he trusteth in thee.
Isaiah 26:3 KJV

Chapter 8

Scattered Clouds, Chance of Showers

The tempest comes out from its chamber, the cold from the driving winds. The breath of God produces ice, and the broad waters become frozen. He loads the clouds with moisture, He scatters His lightning through them. At His direction they swirl around over the face of the whole earth to do whatever He commands them. He brings the clouds to punish people, or to water His earth and show His love.
Job 37:9-13 NIV

"Heart Attack Hotline, we skip a beat for you." This was my telephone greeting when people called the step-down unit to speak to me. I was elated to be on the road to recovery. I was actually feeling and looking better, and I was positive that I was on the mend. I had my loved ones close by, and everyone was also excited about the move from ICU. My parents were scheduled to go home the next day, and I was sure that we could take it from there. Husband was upset with me because of the way I answered the phone. He did not think that it was funny. I was trying to take the light approach to take the edge off of a gloomy situation. Nevertheless, that was all behind me and I was getting ready to go home soon.

    While I was in the ICU, I had developed an unusually high fever that just would not subside. I was given Tylenol 3 and eventually antibiotics upon my request to bring down the fever. It was puzzling to the staff as to why I had a fever. They called in an infectious disease specialist to assess me. This doctor determined that it was safe for me to undergo the first diagnostic test, a cardiac catherization. It was scheduled for Tuesday. I was beginning to believe that there was more to this situation than what met the eye. Why was it so hard for them to figure out what was wrong with me?

I felt badly with the infection in my throat. However, that Monday evening, it started easing up a bit. It was confirmed that I would undergo the testing as scheduled for Tuesday morning. I wasn't thrilled about this testing at all. While in the step-down unit, I had a roommate who had just finished "the test." She had to lie perfectly still for 5 hours with heavy sandbag weights on her legs to stop the bleeding. This certainly did not sound like anything that I wanted to experience. However, everyone assured me that it was just a routine test.

That evening, my roommate was discharged and I was alone. My parents had returned to New York, and visiting hours had ended. With nothing else to do except wait, I watched television. Television was dominated by President Bill Clinton's 1999 State of the Union Address on every channel. Oddly enough I had never been interested in lengthy political speeches but for some reason, I was interested in this one. Since my room was directly in front of the nurse's station, one nurse kept coming in to catch bits and pieces of the speech. After listening to President Clinton ramble on, the final message was that the state of the union was "good".

I was beginning to feel like my state was *good* also. I was preparing to return to my life very soon: my husband, children, job, family and friends. I was beginning to feel like everything was going to be all right. However, somewhere beneath the surface, I was afraid. There was this feeling of *scattered clouds, chance of showers*. A feeling of clouds looming overhead, full, ready to burst forth. The clouds unknowingly foretelling the future and sealing my fate. Clouds disguising the true treachery of the storm that would follow.

That night, sleep would not come; I just could not get comfortable. The room seemed so dark and lonely and it made me uneasy. It felt weird laying there hooked up to a device to monitor my heart. If only that device could see how my heart was really broken. How painful stressed my life had become and how desperate I was for a change. If only it could read the true distress signal. If only the doctors could really heal me everywhere that it hurt. If only they could prescribe a pill that could unblock my emotional and spiritual arteries. If only they could clear away the *scattered clouds and chance of showers*. If only...

Hope deferred makes the heart sick but a longing fulfilled is a tree of life. Proverbs 13:12 NIV

Chapter 9

A Table for One

You prepare a table before me in the presence of my enemies. You anoint my head with oil. My cup overflows. Psalm 23:5 NIV

The table was set and ready just for me. Such care had been given to every detail to make certain that it was just perfect. The instruments were sterilized; the sheets, fresh and clean; every control checked and rechecked. They wheeled me around to the Cardiac Catherization laboratory at about 9:00 a.m., a half hour before the scheduled procedure. It was to be a fairly simple routine procedure, in by 9:30 and out by no later than 10:15.

I was unusually nervous and very afraid. Afraid of what, of dying I guess. I was intimidated by all of the machines and very much in the dark about what was going to take place. My husband had not yet arrived because they came to transport me before the scheduled procedure time.

    I sighed, and I prayed. I prayed, and I sighed. I cried, and I prayed. I prayed, and I cried. I was afraid. Afraid of what, of dying I guess. The lab attendants and nurses were busy preparing for the big event. The doctor was not in the lab when I arrived, but he was on his way. They spoke to me in that pseudo compassionate tone of voice, which said underneath, "Oh girl get over it; it's only a test." What a test it would be, as we soon discovered.

    Just before they administered the sleeping medicine, I jumped up from the table and ran across the hall to the bathroom. I was very afraid. Afraid of what, of dying I guess. I needed to ask God one more time if this was and good thing for me to do, because somehow it just didn't feel right. I also wanted one last chance to see if there was any sign of Husband in the hallway.

Tawanda Prince

Somehow I knew that I should see him before I went under.

So in a small hospital bathroom, I prayed and I cried. I cried and I prayed. I was looking for the answer that I seemed to already know, I had to go through with it. Somehow I knew that my fate had been sealed and that this was no simple, routine test.

Having prayed and cried, I darted back from the bathroom, across the hall from the lab, with my rear end exposed through the opening of the cheap, flimsy hospital gown. I hoisted myself up onto the very narrow, metal table for one. It was quite a balancing act to stay on the table as my future hung in the balance. I was surrounded by beeps, bells, whistles and lights, that they called the Cath lab. To my right was the control room where eventually everything would go out of control. They took turns adjusting dials and pushing buttons, making me feel much like Frankenstein in a scientific experiment.

The red haired nurse rubbed my head to comfort and reassure me. This only made me feel more like a sheep being led to the slaughter. The male attendant was very busy setting things up, and it was agreed that I would need an initial sedative to take the edge off of a very edgy situation. I was afraid. Afraid of what? Afraid of dying I guess.

WAIT! WAIT! WAIT! They needed me to sign a consent form as I lay waiting on the table for one. No time for questions, explanations or options, just sign on the dotted line. The smiling doctor finally entered the scene stage right; it was show time. I fretted, the nurse rubbed, the doctor smile and everything faded to black...

I recall confusion and the feeling of traveling a journey of a thousand miles and back. I remember floating somewhere between consciousness and unconsciousness, between life and death, between never and forever. Suddenly, there was activity all around me. There were people pulling and tugging, prodding and poking. I could vaguely hear what was going on around me as I drifted in and out of reality. What I didn't know was that somewhere in the midst of all of the confusion, things had gone very wrong. In fact, the medical test had come to a screeching halt, but the real "test" for the teacher had just begun.

    I am told that once the sedative had taken effect, they began the catherization procedure. In a perfect world the process begins with inserting a catheter, which is a small plastic tube, through the groin, utilizing that main artery to shoot an iodine dye into the heart. This would allow x-rays of the heart to reveal blockages that may have caused the initial heart attack. However, during my test, the routine process went awry. Apparently when the catheter was inserted, it ripped my left, main artery, causing a massive coronary and death. Yes, DEATH!

Yea though I walk through the valley of the shadow of death, I will fear no evil for Thou art with me.

***Thy rod and Thy staff they comfort me.
Psalms 23:4 KJV***

CODE BLUE! CODE BLUE! CODE BLUE! In medical terminology, I coded and needed to be resuscitated by a defibrillator to jump start my heart. In laymen's terms, I needed to be brought back to life. Simply put, I needed a miracle, and fast. It is good to know that God does not require advance notice. Miracles are often granted upon immediate request. The medical team was able to jump start my heart, this being the first of an out-of-this-world series of miracles.

Once they had me stabilized, the decision was made to transport me over to Washington Medical Center, in Washington, D.C., via Medi-vac. I can recall the rush of cold, January wind whipping underneath that cheap, flimsy hospital gown, as they wheeled my table for one to the waiting helicopter. I can recall the loud sounds from the helicopter being muffled as they placed covering over my ears. Through it all, God

Tawanda Prince

blessed me with the miracle of sleep and I don't remember any more of the air trip but I am sure flying from Southern, Maryland to North West Washington, D.C. is no joy ride, when one is on life support.

Chapter 10

The Heart of the Matter

For I know the plans I have for you, declares the LORD, plans to prosper you and not to harm you, plans to give you hope and a future. Then you will call on Me and come and pray to Me, and I will listen to you. You will seek Me and find Me when you seek Me with all your heart. Jeremiah 27:11-13 NIV

Washington Medical Center was a place that I had only heard about. It was a place for sick people, old people, dying people, but certainly not a place for me. How could I end up in a place like this? Wasn't I fine just a week ago? Hadn't I just returned to work from maternity leave? Didn't I just have a baby two months ago? Wasn't I only 37 years old? Weren't my future plans waiting to be fulfilled? So how did I end up like this at Washington Medical Center?

Answers to these questions evaded me, as I lay struggling for life, on a gurney in Washington Medical Center. I arrived there still unconscious from the trauma at Southern Medical Hospital. Now having suffered one mild heart attack and one massive heart attack, I was on life support and my survival was unpredictable.

Family, friends and loved ones gathered for support and perhaps to say goodbye. Husband was by my side concerned for my well-being and afraid of being left alone. Jen, Alva and Marla stood by my bedside looking at a fellow teacher learning about one of life's harsh lessons. They were standing by when I awoke in Washington Medical Center searching for answers to questions that only God knew.

But when He, the spirit of truth comes, He will lead you into all truth. John 16:13 NIV

There is a big difference between fact and truth. The facts said that at the age of 37, I had suffered two heart attacks, died once and my heart was so damaged that chances of recovery were slim at best. But at the heart of the matter was the **TRUTH**. That **TRUTH** was that all power is in Jesus.

I am the way, the TRUTH and the life and no one comes to the Father except through Me. John 14:6NIV

In the flesh, my body had failed me. My heart had weakened under the attack. The enemy was trying to take me down by waging an attack on my physical heart. But at the heart of the matter was God. The word of God says in Isaiah 54:17, *"No weapon that is formed against you will prevail."* **(NIV)** No weapon, means not heart attacks; not imperfect medical equipment, not faulty medical procedures, not incompetent medical staff, not even death.

The facts said, I didn't stand much of a chance. But the **TRUTH** said, ***"Low I am with you always even unto the ends of the world." Matthew 28:20 KJV*** It certainly felt like the end of the world to me, for it was indeed the end of life as I had come to know it. As I lay there unable to speak, or even breathe on my own, I had only to trust in the **TRUTH**.

I lay there looking up at Husband, Jen and Alva by my bedside, medical personnel busy all around me, tubes and hoses plugged in as I drifted back into reality. From my vantage point, the emergency room in Washington Medical Center was a hub of healing and care. Get-'em-in; fix-'em-up; ship-'em-out; operating much like a well-oiled machine, until a case comes along that pauses their routine. It's that case that causes them to stop and scratch their heads, fully aware of the power of a force far greater than themselves.

So there I lay. I immediately asked to write since verbal communication was impossible while on life support. The first question that I asked was, "Am I dying?" The answer they gave was, "NO." Next, I asked, "Am I on life support?" They answered, "NO." Finally I asked, "When is dinner?"

Everyone broke into a laughter that expressed mutual agreement that underneath all of this destruction there is Tawanda. I had been known for being overly concerned about mealtime, and even in my critical state, I knew that I had missed a meal or two.

The medical team was astonished by my ordinary reactions during such an extraordinary event. What they didn't know was that I serve an extraordinary God. A God who's **TRUTH** transcends all factual reality. A God who assures us that it is not over until He says it is over. The **TRUTH** was, it had just begun. In fact, there were more head turning, mind boggling, death-defying, life-transforming miracles yet in store for me.

The doctor asked me, with a bit of astonishment, "Do you know what you have gone through?" My unspoken response was, "Do you know who I am in Christ?" The next question that I wrote was, "When can I get the tube out of my throat?" After all, I had lots of eating and talking to do. Little did I know that the removal of the tube would be quite an ordeal. The reason I didn't quite understand was because I was unconscious when the tube was inserted, so I was spared the agony of having a foreign object shoved passed the organs in the throat and chest. However, I would be awake when they pulled the tube back through the same pathway. Although it was going to be painful and uncomfortable, it was better than the discomfort of being restricted by having the tube in my throat.

Once they decided to remove the tube, I had a job to do. I would have to prove to them that I could make it on my own. I didn't know how difficult that would be. Immediately after the tube was removed, they asked me to speak. I gleefully blurted out, *"Thank you Jesus."* Everyone laughed and they all let out that same awkward sigh of relief that I had heard when I woke up.

It was a roller coaster ride filled with emotional and physical peaks and valleys. A ray of hope would then be quickly overshadowed by the facts of my deteriorating condition. The facts were that not many people survive two heart attacks within less than a week. Thank God I was standing on the **TRUTH** instead of the facts. I was standing for myself and for others to see the glory of God through the miracles in my life. Now was not the time to weaken. God said,

Stand firm then, with the belt of truth buckled around your waist. Ephesians 6:14 NIV

Chapter 11

Knock, Knock. Who's There?

At this my heart pounds and leaps from its place. Listen! Listen to the roar of His voice to the rumbling that comes from His mouth. He unleashes His lightning beneath the whole heaven and sends it to the ends of the earth. After that comes the sound of His roar; He thunders with His majestic voice. When His voice resounds, He holds nothing back. God's voice thunders in marvelous ways; He does great things beyond our understanding. Job 37:1-5

Knock, knock. Who's There?

Thunder. Thunder Who? Thunder knocking at your heart.

There was no way that I could know just what was in store for me. I was vaguely aware of what was going on. However, I knew enough to understand that this was serious, very serious. The looks of fear and concern on the faces in the room warned of danger; careful whispers spoke of trouble; curious eyes searched for answers.

Knock, knock. Who's there? Thunder. Thunder Who? Thunder Knocking at your heart.

The medical team allowed my visitors to stay for just a short while. My condition was critical and I needed intensive care. Dr. Ling ordered the visitors to leave the room for a minute so that the nurse could change me into another clean, cheap, flimsy hospital gown, and prepare me for the dinner that I requested. The care plan was to let me rest for the evening and resume treatment in the morning. It seemed as though everything shifted to one side of the boat as they all left the room. I was alone, afraid because so much had already happened, and I was uncertain of my future.

As the nurse closed the door, a strange feeling swept over me. I felt myself entering that dark place yet again. The nurse went about trying to make me more comfortable. She attempted to clean me up and change my gown. I resisted because I didn't feel well. I asked her to just let me be. She assured me that this would make me feel belter. I acquiesced, but I really didn't want to.

Knock, knock. Who's there? Thunder. Thunder who? Thunder knocking at your heart.

My chest hurt. It was that pain that I had recently become familiar with when I met **JUMBO**, once you experience you never forget it. The pressure in the middle intensified. The waves of excruciating pain overtook my body. My mind screamed, "NO!" My body and **JUMBO** screamed, "YES!"

I notified the nurse of the pain. She quickly assessed my condition on the pain scale of 1-10. When I answered, 11, she immediately called the doctor because there was no time to waste. We all knew what was happening. I was having a third heart attack. Suddenly my faith was taken to another level. I was sure this time that I was going to die. Although I knew that God could do anything, I thought this was surely the end.

After informing my loved ones, they rushed me to the Cardiac Catherization Laboratory once again. That was certainly not my favorite place to be. However, it was the only means by which they could determine what was going on with my heart.

Three heart attacks were beyond anyone's scope of reasoning. Surviving one attack was incredible; two, amazing, and three was miraculous. We were all praying for a miracle.

The pain intensified. I had never really heard many people talk about the pain of a heart attack. Although the whole experience differs from person to person, pain is the common denominator. It is the type of pain that you cannot touch. It grips deep, down on the inside, with no way to relieve the pressure. The PAIN...

    It **PRESSES!**

        It **STABS!**

It **PUSHES!**

        It **GRIPS!**

    It **SQUEEZES!**

It **TWISTS!**

        It **PIERCES!**

    It **PULSATES!**

      It **HURTS!**

For some it hurts unto death. For some the pain passes through, much like a raging storm, with lightning, **THUNDER**, cumulous clouds and rain that rages and ravages mercilessly. For some, the storm passes over.

Chapter 12

The Storm is Passing Over

In the six hundredth year of Noah's life, on the seventeenth day of the second month-on that day all the springs of the great deep burst forth, and the floodgates of the heavens were opened. And rain fell on the earth forty days and forty nights.
Genesis 7:11-12

As they wheeled me from the Catherization lab to the operating room, I was painfully aware of my circumstances. I was facing a storm that only God could control. My parents had not yet returned from New York, which left me without a chance to say goodbye to them. Husband and Jen followed alongside me on the gurney for as far as they were allowed to. I recall feeling that this was "IT." This was finally "IT." I felt that I had reached the end of my journey on this side of heaven. A huge wave of fear consumed me, for I realized that I may not be prepared to die.

I searched my mental index of the Bible recognizing that I didn't know what steps to take. Was being saved truly enough? Was accepting the gift of salvation all I really needed to do to make it in? What about all of the rotten things that I had said and done? Was that going to send me to hell? What if I had been given some faulty information? Just what were the steps I needed to take? Is this really IT? The teacher in me just knew that there must be some other steps. Finally, in a silent prayer, I asked God for his forgiveness for the sins that I had committed, confessing to him that I really didn't know what one needed to do to prepare to die.

In a final human attempt to cover myself, as I lay on the gurney, I told Jen to apologize to Alva if I had offended her at work. It's funny how we develop a taste for humble pie when we think that we are going to die. Jen cried and assured me that it was all "o.k." We all exchanged sentiments of "I love you" and "I'll see you later," and I was thinking either here or on the other side. Then it was operating time and I entered the forbidden zone with the heading "Authorized Personnel Only."

My heart was in bad condition. I had suffered three heart attacks, and the attempted angioplasty, done in Washington Medical Center, had failed. Angioplasty is a procedure by which an attempt is made to open the blocked arteries by inserting a balloon to open up the passageway. Having the balloon in place keeps the arteries from closing up which allow for better blood flow. However, this procedure didn't work for me; my heart was too damaged at this point.

I remember looking up at Dr. Orzo, as we were introduced on the operating table. He explained that I would need double bypass surgery. This is a surgical operation that involves removal of one of the body's major veins, in my case, the right leg from the groin to just below the knee. Then, that vein is used to re-route blood flow, or bypass the blocked or damaged areas, to the healthy functioning areas. Double bypass is when this procedure is performed on two blocked or damaged arteries in the heart. I recall saying to myself, "So this is what open-heart surgery is." The time had come so I said another quick prayer, just to cover myself, as they placed the mask over my face. Counting backwards from 100, 99, 98, 97, 96, 95...*fade to black*.

    The storm was raging, and like any storm transformation is imminent. Nothing encounters a storm without experiencing change. The storm was raging in both my physical and spiritual heart. I was in a place of desolation and in need of reformation. I truly needed a change of heart. While the doctors performed a physical bypass, God was performing a spiritual bypass.

    God needed to clear the blocked passageway in my heart, where sin and disobedience were blocking my blessing flow. He would need to re-route the blood flow and infuse it with the blood of Jesus. Open heart surgery would involve a cleansing and purifying process only possible in the hands of the Master Surgeon. It was necessary to strengthen and reinforce the damaged areas of my heart with what was good. Then I would be able to stand and withstand future storms.

Now the springs of the deep and the floodgates of the heavens had been closed, and the rain had stopped falling from the sky. The water receded steadily from the earth. Genesis 8:1-3 NIV

Chapter 13

The Awakening

There is a time for everything and a season for every activity under the heavens: a time to be born and a time to die. Ecclesiastes 3: 1-2 NIV

I awakened from a sleep like no other, eyes heavy and body unfamiliar. I saw, yet I didn't see; I heard, yet I didn't hear. I believed, yet I didn't believe. *White.* All I saw was *white.* All I smelled was *white.* All I tasted was *white.* I thought to myself, as I transition from *white* to black, "This white over my head is not a cloud, and it's not a coffin; I must be alive." It was my awakening.

I awakened from a new sleep and yet an old sleep. A sleep with promise, a sleep of transformation. A journey ending and a journey beginning. The passing into a season of change. As I came into awareness of my condition, I recognized that nothing was as it had been, and it would not be the same again.

    The phones were ringing and the nurses were moving about, responding to bells, whistles, and beeps. My hearing was sharpening with each unfamiliar sound. I listened to try to figure out what was happening with me. My hands and feet were bound, and there were tubes and hoses running from every area of my body. My very existence was wrapped in pain, yet somewhere in the supernatural, there was healing.

    After I awakened, I tried desperately to get the attention of the nurses because I wanted them to know that I was alive. I moaned and groaned as much as I could with the obstruction in my throat. I was on life support and there was an endotracheal tube in my mouth. It was so uncomfortable with all of the tubes infused in my body, especially the one sewn into my neck.

    I ached and I longed for the comfort of a familiar face. I longed to see my loved ones. On the phone, directly across from my bed, I could hear the nurse responding to questions about me from family members. I was aware that my condition was extremely serious. I was gagging and choking yet unable to utter a word because I had the ventilator tube in my throat. I then gestured to the nurse that I wanted to communicate by writing. She was hesitant to untie my hands because she feared that I would attempt to remove the tubes that were in place. I reassured her that I would not and she allowed me to write on a pad as best I could. My question, "What happened to me?"

I waited for what seemed a lifetime for a familiar face. Mom…Dad…Husband…pastor…doctor…I ached and I waited. Finally, I saw my parents walk through the door with a look of fear. Afraid. Afraid of what? Afraid of seeing death and afraid of seeing a life shattered, I imagine. They trembled as they walked with trepidation towards my bed. Their eyes searched for what had been lost. Yet, I could see in their eyes hope for what was to come. Their hearts were broken yet rejoiced, for there had been an awakening. Tears of joy and tears of sorrow that only a parent can know when their only child's spirit has been broken. As they stood and watched, they believed that God was with me.

I ached and my heart was broken. I cried and I screamed yet unable to make a sound with the tube in my throat. I was afraid, very afraid. Afraid of seeing death and afraid of facing life shattered. It was an awakening like no other.

My bed was nearest to the doors of the recovery room which would be my home until later that day. My husband appeared through those doors wearing a face of fear and helplessness. My heart rejoiced yet there was the foreboding feeling that I was in deep waters. He could barely stand to look at me, so overwhelmed by my appearance. I knew that I would need to lean on him in the days to come, but I saw in his eyes that at the moment he was sinking sand.

My body ached. I couldn't speak, eat, move, or breathe, yet I was alive and rivers of hope flowed from heart to heart. The minutes marched like wooden soldiers as I endured my stay in recovery. The process was almost unbearable. Several attempts to remove me from life support resulted in, "Not yet ready," because my blood gas level needed to reach a certain reading before I could be taken off of the ventilator. So I ached and I waited.

Perhaps, the recovery room should be aptly renamed the "awakening room." For it was the place where I awakened to face the wreckage that remained after my storm had ended. It was the place where I began to gather the fragments of a broken body and shattered life. It was the place where I awakened to face my uncertain future. It was where I discovered the difference between waking up and awakening. I had an awakening!

But He said to me, 'My grace is sufficient for you, My power is made perfect in your weakness.' 2 Corinthians 12:9

Chapter 14

The Eye of the Storm

And God said, "Let there be light," and there was light. God saw that the light was good, and He separated the light from the darkness. God called the light day and the darkness He called night. And there was evening, and there was morning-the first day. Genesis 1: 3-5 NIV

At approximately 2:00 p.m., January 21, 1999, I was transported from "The Awakening Room" to a room in the cardiac step-down unit. My family had gathered around me and each one breathed a sigh of relief because we were seemingly in the eye of the storm. However, everyone knew that although a storm may last for a brief time recovery and reconstruction could take forever.

Tawanda Prince

They stood guard as I was transported from the awakening room, to the hallway, to the elevator, to the hallway, and finally to the room. As we approached my room, I struggled to keep from slipping back into nothingness. It was difficult for me to make sense out of all that had occurred. I only knew that I was broken. Bits and pieces lay scattered where my life had once been. The remnants and fragments were barely recognizable and seemingly irreparable.

Again, there were more questions than answers as the gurney moved me toward the next phase of my destiny. I had traveled down the passageway of change, and I was left to pick up the pieces. It was impossible to know exactly what lie ahead, but I knew it would be a time of gathering and a time of harvesting. It would take miracle after miracle to inch along the path to wholeness. For everyone knows that although a storm may last for just a brief time, recovery and restoration could take longer than forever.

Tawanda Prince

When I finally made it to my room, it was as though I had traveled through two lifetimes. My family stood around my bed as if positioned to protect me from any further hurt or harm. I believe they even wanted to shield me from my own reality. Each face reflected the struggle between fear and hope, fear of the worst and hope for the best. They tried so desperately to pretend that all was well, but it was obvious that all was not well. For my parents who had not had a chance to see me before the surgery, it was like a brand new day.

My room number was 4E-3B, and my bed was near the window. Outside of my window there was a wall. Across from that wall there was another wall. Beyond that wall there was a world. The first wall blocked part of my view. It was symbolic of my position at the time. There was life beyond that wall. Although I could not see it, I had to trust that it was there. I remember eventually hating that wall. It blocked my view and made me feel boxed in. The wall symbolized the stumbling blocks that would need to be used as stepping stones in my immediate future. It also reminded me of the obstacles that would lead to opportunities, just as the raindrops would lead to the rainbow.

That first hour in the room was the settling in period. We all faced the fact that recovery would be a long and arduous process, requiring many baby steps before I could make leaps and bounds. Dr. Ling, my hospital appointed and God anointed cardiologist, came by to pay me a visit to discuss the details of my condition with me and my family. Dr. Ling served as a messenger from above. He was delighted to actually meet me and my family, and was eager to share his amazement at what had occurred. My series of events were so incredibly outrageous that he joked that my ordeal had probably taken years off of his life.

Dr. Ling informed us that not only had I been rushed into surgery as a result of the three heart attacks, but during the bypass, I had suffered another massive cardiac arrest and died. Yes DIED! Again! I had died again for the second time that day and the **"CODE BLUE"** had been signaled. Once again, God's hand of mercy had restored me. Even the doctor had to acknowledge the obvious miracle working hand of God on my life. He stopped by to let me know that I was truly a miracle. He took no credit for himself, but acknowledged that he was merely an instrument under divine order.

It only takes a moment for one's life to be completely changed. In the twinkling of an eye a transformation can take place. It is at these times when we clearly see that God truly has the whole world in his hands. He is really the true potter, and we are the clay.

So, there I was a lump of clay on the "Potter's Wheel" awaiting complete transformation. Going into the surgery, I was told that I would need a double bypass because of the damage sustained from the first three heart attacks. As it turned out, with four arteries needing repair, I underwent a quadruple bypass as a result of that fourth and final cardiac arrest.

It is important to note the difference between a heart attack and a cardiac arrest. A heart attack occurs when the heart resets its electrical pattern and skips or misses heart beats. Cardiac arrest occurs when the heart beat is gone the heart stops completely. Most often when this occurs the heart is unable to reset without defibrillation. It was truly a miracle that I was alive after sustaining such trauma to the heart and to my body.

So as a lump of clay on the "Potter's Wheel," awaiting complete transformation, I was just passing through. Passing form dark to light, from old to new, from raindrops to rainbow. Although I did not know what my future held, I knew the one who held my future in his hands. There was great darkness in the room that afternoon. Fear was hovering like a dark cloud overhead, and my family and I were all so unsure of the future. It was impossible to imagine life beyond this storm.

My cousin Honcho and his wife were waiting for me to come out of recovery, and I recall passing them in the hallway as I was transported to my room. Upon arrival in my room, I was so thirsty. The surgery had left me dry. I was only allowed ice chips and small doses of liquids. My father kept feeding me little sips of juice as my sentiments echoed Jesus' final words, "I thirst."

I was still hooked up to post surgery equipment, and the tubes were running from various parts of my chest and abdomen. It was almost impossible to breathe or move without pain. Bandages and blood were all I could see as I looked down at my body. I ached and I felt like my body had been torn in half. I later discovered that during the surgery, my body had been cut in half and put back together.

During the bypass surgery, the center bone of my chest cavity had been sawed in half and propped open. This allowed the surgeons access to my heart for the surgery. My right leg had been cut from my groin down to three inches below my knee to remove the saphenous vein. This is the long vein down the inside of the thigh that was divided and placed inside my heart to permit blood flow and "by-pass" the damaged areas. Additionally, there were two wires hanging out from the center of my abdomen. These wires were in place as a precaution in case I needed a pacemaker during the post-surgery period. The wires were later removed as the pacemaker was not needed at that time. Also, I was hooked up to a heart monitor, oxygen tank, and another machine that drained excess blood and fluid from my heart to prevent me from drowning in my own juice. To top it all off, my hair was a matted mess; my body and breath stank, and I was hungry. But to my family I looked like an angel. For I had seen death from the victim's vantage point, yet I was now alive and looking like hope. I may have been unappealing to the human eye, but spiritual eyes saw a lump of clay that God was still molding.

Tawanda Prince

Yea though I walk through the valley of the shadow of death, I will fear no evil for thou art with me. Thy rod and thy staff they comfort me. Psalms 23:4

Indeed God's staff had comforted me. The team of nurses, doctors, assistants, lab technicians, transporters, Medi-vac pilots, custodians, cooks, and even administration were all used by God to comfort and care for me. As I passed through the valley of the shadow of death, they all played a vital part in ushering me into the light of a new day and a new life.

I was uncomfortable in the bed. It was almost impossible to find a position that would accommodate all of my apparatuses without extreme pain. However, I was happy to be out of recovery, off of life support and able to have my hands and feet unbound. It was quite an effort for me to talk, but I couldn't keep quiet. I joked as much as I could and rejoiced with my family about my miracles. I struggled to make sense out of all that I had encountered. My memory was initially fuzzy, and it all seemed like a horrible dream. This could not have been happening to me, my mind reasoned. As my life was now so unfamiliar, Tawanda was being redefined, reconstructed and recreated. The biggest question in my mind was, "Will I make it through all of this?" That seemed to be the question in the eyes of everyone who stood around my bedside. The unspeakable and unthinkable was foremost in all of our minds but we clung to the hope that spewed forth with each breath that I took. Yes, we rejoiced because there had been an awakening.

    The highlight of the afternoon came when my body told me that it was time to use the bathroom. In spite of it all, my body struggled to resume normal function. We called for the nurse to help me and she informed me that I would need to take my first walk over to the bathroom. Everyone winced at the thought of me enduring so much pain while walking across the room. Since my bed was near the window, it was going to be a very long walk. The nurse assisted me out of the bed and my family unsuccessfully attempted to hold back the tears as I struggled to make that journey. As I dragged my damaged body inching along, the nurse pulled along the machine that was draining the fluid and the intravenous pump. Needless to say, it took me a very long time to get to the other side of the room. Judging from the facial expressions in the room, my painstaking efforts were felt by everyone.

Walking was intensely painful. I could not imagine ever walking normally, free of pain again. The tears I cried did not clearly express the depth of the pain and discomfort I was experiencing. Additionally, I was dealing with the fear factor. I reasoned that if it was such a challenge just to walk to the bathroom, how was I going to walk back into my life? Walking was such a simple thing, now extremely complicated in the eye of the storm. These were the first of many steps that I had to take toward recovery, and no one else in the room could take them for me.

After I finally made it to the bathroom and sat down, I wondered how I would make it back to the bed. Once again, those facial expressions told me that everyone else in the room was wondering the same thing. Performing the task at hand was no easy feat. Each movement required me to push pass the constrictions of pain and allow my body to begin to function in the perfection in which God created it to function. The medical team was ecstatic that my body functions were returning to normal. This was the green light indicator to them that healing had begun and that my body was attempting to jump-start itself. I felt like a child going to the potty for the first time. **APPLAUSE! APPLAUSE! APPLAUSE!**

As I struggled back to the bed, the nurse informed me that I needed to be weighed. It was important for my weight to be carefully monitored for detection of body fluid increase or decrease and potential heart malfunction. Although this may sound like a simple task, nothing is simple when your chest has been sawed in half. This process required me to lift myself and all of my equipment up on a scale and hold steady until my weight was recorded. This was more than I wanted to deal with at the present time, but nevertheless, I managed to accomplish the task. Exhausted, I made my way back to the bed with clear intentions of not drinking any more liquids in order to decrease the possibility of going to the bathroom any time soon.

   Then the time drew nigh for my family to leave. It had been a long day, which seemed more like a lifetime, and everyone was exhausted. For we had all been beyond and back in the past 24 hours, and we needed rest. But I was afraid, very afraid. Afraid of what? Afraid of dying I guess. I did not want them to leave me there all alone. Recent experiences had proven that every time they left me, something happened to me. Eventually they all left except for one. God always has a ram in the bush. My friend Kandace lingered afterwards to look after me. Since she works in the medical field, she was still dressed in her hospital scrubs. This enabled her to blend in with the rest of the medical team and no one asked her to leave. She stayed and prayed with me and helped me calm down. She sat right next to my bed and held my weak hand until I fell asleep.

I had made it through the first day of my new life.

He stilled the storm to a whisper. The waves of the sea were hushed. Psalm 107:29 NIV

Chapter 15

There is Power in the Blood

But if we walk in the light, as He is in the light, we have fellowship with one another, and the blood of Jesus, His Son, purifies us from all sin. 1 John 1:7 NIV

On day two following the surgery, the reality had really begun to sink in. It was clear that *thunder had knocked at my heart* and the storm was not yet over. This was the day that the medical team tried to figure out what to do with me next. Some were still scratching their heads amazed by God's miracles in me. There was testing, testing and more testing in order to determine my treatment plan. One such test revealed that there was a problem with my blood. Oh no, not the blood! Oh yes, the blood!

I was unaware that I had previously received two blood transfusions during surgery. Now, I needed two more transfusions to enable recovery. My mind instantly filled with a barrage of questions and intense fear. For it was no secret that some people have contracted AIDS through blood transfusions so I questioned just how safe it was. At this point, I was still clueless about the treatment of my condition. Exactly what was my condition? In basic terms, my heart was broken, and I needed **the blood**.

Blood is the center of all life. Without blood there is no life. Without His **blood** there is no eternal life in heaven. **Blood. Blood** bath, **blood**line, **blood** pressure, **blood** poisoning, **blood** relations, **blood**shed, **blood**shot, **blood** stream, **blood** sucker, **blood** thirsty and **blood** vessel. Suddenly **blood** took on a whole new meaning.

I anguished over accepting the two forthcoming transfusions. I was also creeped out with the thought of someone else's blood already running through my veins. One of the nurses on duty posed the deciding question to me. Choice A was to accept the blood and live.

Choice B was to not accept the blood and die. It quickly became painfully evident that I would have to accept the blood.

This day I call the heavens and the earth as witnesses against you that I have set before you life and death, blessings and curses. Now choose life, so that you and your children may live and that you may love the Lord your God, listen to His voice, and hold fast to Him. Deuteronomy 30: 19-20a NIV

    A blood transfusion is a relatively simple procedure that yields miraculous results. The twelve hour process involves pumping a bag of blood into your veins through an intravenous line. This process mixes the new blood with your blood to strengthen your system and extend your life.

    So it is with the blood of Jesus. Through Christ's **bloodshed** and death on the cross, burial and resurrection, we experience a **blood transfusion** or

blood bath. His precious blood is mixed with our blood to cleanse us of ***blood poisoning*** from our sins as he offers forgiveness. The goal is to strengthen our system and give us eternal life and a new ***bloodline.*** Without His cleansing *blood* we would die from the elevated ***blood pressure*** of guilt and shame. We cannot survive without **"the blood"** because both our bodies and souls are ***blood vessels*** that are ***blood thirsty.***

When you were dead in your sins and in the uncircumcision of your flesh, God made you alive with Christ. He forgave us all our sins, having canceled the charge of our legal indebtedness, which stood against us and condemned us; He has taken it away, nailing it to the cross. And having disarmed the powers and authorities, He made a public spectacle of them, triumphing over them by the cross. Colossians 2: 13-15 NIV

So I agreed to accept the blood, but I did not have complete peace about my decision. After visiting hours ended, somewhere around midnight, a nurse came to set up the transfusion. She explained that I would receive one bag of blood during the night and the second bag would be given to me in the morning. She could see that I was upset about the transfusion. I was fretting and crying, and I am sure my facial expression read, "Oh no, not the blood." I told her about my concerns regarding "the blood" and all that I had been through in the past week. I expressed my confusion about past events and my uncertain future.

  The nurse listened with compassion. Then with a familiar Caribbean accent, she spoke what God laid on her heart. Her accent was particularly comforting to me because she sounded like my grandmother Trudy. She explained that I really did not have any other viable options, I had to choose life. After all that had happened during this storm, now the decision rested in my hands. I had a choice, and I would be held accountable for that choice. I had to make a decision in faith. The world told me that receiving the blood could be a bad choice. The Word told me that there is no other choice but to receive **the blood**. The world told me that I had no power. The Word told me that there is power in **the blood,** and that I too possessed that power through Jesus Christ. It is a choice that everyone must make to receive **the blood** or refuse it. The consequence of not receiving **the blood** is death but the reward of receiving the blood is eternal life.

There is Power in the Blood

Lewis E. Jones (1899)

Would you be free from your burden of sin
There is power in the blood, power in the blood
Would you over evil a victory win
There's wonderful power in the blood
There is power, power wonder working power
In the blood of the lamb
There is power, power wonder working power
In the precious blood of the lamb

Tawanda Prince

With an unconventional gesture, before the nurse administered the blood, she prayed with me and over me. She prayed that the blood flowing from the bag into my veins would be the blood of Jesus. Instantly, it was well with my soul. She connected the bag of blood to the intravenous line in my left arm. As the blood flowed I drifted off to sleep. It was amazing that God had sent this saint to administer the blood and to minister to my spirit. My faith was being fine-tuned and I was forced to trust on a level that I had never trusted before. God was making me "choose life" not just live. That nurse was a reminder that God is who He says in His word that He is and that I must be who I say I am according to my faith in Christ. God used that nurse to usher me to a higher faith level. I realized I could no longer be a victim in this storm. God showed me that nurse was His agent. Oddly enough, I never saw that "nurse" again during my stay in the hospital.

The precious **blood** of Jesus will never lose its power. Perhaps you have never accepted this gift of salvation and eternal life through the blood of Jesus, now is an acceptable time.

Without the shedding of blood there can be no forgiveness. Hebrew 9:22

(To receive salvation see Author's Note at the back of the book)

Chapter 16

Family Reunion

Behold, I stand at the door, and knock: if any man hear My voice, and open the door, I will come in to him, and will sup with him, and he with Me. Revelations 3:20 KJV

By Saturday, January 24, 1999, the news of my situation had spread. No internet, no press conference and no all-points bulletin, just simply word of mouth. Everyone was shocked and horrified by my ordeal and fearful about my chances of survival. That day, the visitors rolled in one by one, and I was surprised by some but elated by all.

It seemed that everyone came at the same time. Fellow teachers, Marva, Vee, and LeShaun came to cheer me. Also much to my surprise, my current and former principals, came. Even two of my students Kennedy and MyKeisha came. We all laughed as my students reminded me that I was "looking crazy." They had never seen me out of my teacher persona. My hair was a mess, my breath stank, and I still had on that cheap, ugly, flimsy hospital gown that exposed my rear end when I walked. Though they all tried to hide it, the same look of fear and pity was etched on each face. Although I was growing tired from all of the visitors, I did not want anyone to leave. Of course my parents and my husband were there by my side.

In the midst of it all, everyone recognized that the only way to healing and wholeness was to turn to God. It was obvious that God's miraculous power was the only thing that was going to bring restoration to my life and to my family. The Principals lead the prayer circle. They prayed for God to continue the good work that he had begun in me. As we all united in prayer, God's spirit filled the room. Emotions ran high and fear wrestled against faith in predicting the final outcome. No one could see past the moment, but we all clung to hope.

My friends Adelle and Marty stopped by and brought me a Bible. It was a small Bible that I could carry in my purse when needed. God used these two to equip me for the ministry that lay ahead. After coming through the storm, they thought it would be wise to carry God's Word on my journey. Adelle had known for quite some time that God had called me to the ministry so this was their send off to my mission.

Although each visitor was special in their own way, my two favorite people in this world finally came to see me. J.C. and Sadie arrived in the midst of all of the chaos. The room was packed and the buzz was loud in the air. Words cannot express the emotions that I felt upon seeing my babies. I was overjoyed to see them but heartbroken because I could not embrace or hold them without assistance. J.C. was afraid of the hospital and all of the care apparatus. I did not look like myself with the oxygen tube in my nose, not to mention my hair was looking crazy. He walked slowly to me with the innate wisdom of caution that a child has when something is wrong. He stood in front of me, and I held on as best I could. It hurt me that I could not pick him up or draw him close to me. The tears in the room began to flow. Then it was Sadie's turn. The family gently placed my baby in my lap supporting her with their own hands. I couldn't hold her, but I could touch her. There is something miraculous in the touch and smell of a baby. I cried unable to express my true emotions with regards to my children. I loved them beyond measure, and I needed them to help facilitate my healing. Everyone in the room knew that J.C. and Sadie were the inspiration for my will to live. I was not just fighting for my own life, I was fighting for theirs.

It was a brief visit. It is difficult to determine whether my heart ached more before the children arrived or after they left. Such emptiness and brokenness prevailed because I knew that the road to recovery and discovery would be a long one. Nonetheless, I knew I would recover to become who God wanted me to be. Obviously, I was Husband's wife;

J.C. and Sadie's mother; Roz and Al's daughter; and even Kennedy and MyKeisha's teacher, but just who was God calling me out to be? It was clear that I had an assignment and God was sending me on my mission. In one aspect, I could not even imagine climbing the stairs up to my bedroom in my house, but I knew that once released, I would have to follow "Mission Possible."

Without fail, whenever one is called by God, the enemy springs into action. Mr. Fear was ever present riding my back like a thief in the night. The enemy was positioned to steal, kill, and destroy; ready to rob me of my purpose and steal my thunder. Ominous storm clouds threatened to destroy my world. This enemy, Mr. Fear, was determined to kill my body, spirit, dream mission and vision. I found myself trapped by fear: fear of death; fear of life and fear of failure. Most of all, what I really feared was becoming who God wanted me to be.

THUNDER! THUNDER had knocked at the door of my heart so many times. **THUNDER** rattling in the distance growing into a ferocious rumble. **THUNDER** was knocking again after the storm, undeniably resounding my name. **THUNDER** beckoning me to come out from among them. **THUNDER** proclaiming the ending of one storm and the beginning of another. **THUNDER** accompanied by lightening showcasing teasing glimpses of the glory that lie ahead. **THUNDER** knocking at my heart, refusing to accept "no" for and answer again. **THUNDER**, loud, shaking, roaring, rousing, rumbling, resounding **THUNDER!**

    On that day in the hospital, God sent many loved ones by to remind me of his love and the power of love. Love is the transforming factor. Because I had love, I had hope. Hope for a better tomorrow. Hope to complete the missions that lie ahead. Hope which reaffirmed my will to live. I realized it is that will that God desires. He wants our will to trust and submit to his will. For some, that comes relatively easy; for others it takes **THUNDER!**

Chapter 17

Homeward Bound

But I will restore you to health and heal your wounds, declares the Lord. Jeremiah 30:17 NIV

I remained in the hospital for three more days. Each day began with the hope of going home. I was missing my personal space. A space I had so often taken for granted. I longed for my house and my home. A house is a place that holds our things. A home is the space that holds our heart. Although I was eager, I had a heavy load that I had carried before the "twister", and presently I was unable to even carry myself. My babies needed me, my husband needed me, and my students needed me. Just what would I be able to give them, I questioned myself and God.

The three remaining days in the hospital brought more questions than answers. The wall outside of my window reminded me that I was stuck between a brick and a hard place. During that time, my physical strength was slowly building but not my confidence. We all had great concern about my recovery. It would be a long road and the doctors cautioned against overzealous expectations. They explained that I would need to define a "new normal." This meant that life as we had known it had ended. It would be a new day when I returned home and that frightened me and the people in my world.

As part of the exit process, I was required to attend a class on adjusting to life after a heart attack and heart surgery. Husband and my parents also had to attend the class because recovery would require a family effort. The nurse wheeled me to the room where the class was being held. Upon entering the classroom, reality hit me like a ton of bricks. There I sat in a room full of heart afflicted elderly people. What a twisted reality. It reminded me that two months prior, I sat in a similar classroom at Sacred Cross Hospital in a post baby delivery class. I had gone from having a baby to having a heart attack in just two short months, and I was in a dark place. I had gone from bringing forth life to adjusting to rebuilding life after death.

The class was chock full of information on everything from how to care for the incisions to what to eat and drink. As they droned on, the voices in my head were screaming, "NO, THIS ISN'T HAPPENING TO ME." I realized that I had become a heart attack "survivor." Yes a survivor! This class was teaching me how to survive after such a traumatic event. It was equipping me for recovery after the storm of a SHATTERED life. I looked at the other patients in the room, then at my family and then at myself. I could still hear the "thunder" knocking, and I began to cry. I was grieving for what had been lost. On that table, TAWANDA had truly died. Thunder had destroyed the life that I had known. The old had passed away, and I had to learn to live with what was left. What had taken 37 years to build was now in ruins due to a storm that swept through in a flash. Gone, but not forgotten.

There was really no way to prepare to go home. No class could describe what the transition would really be like. As we left the class, my family all shared the same feeling of being overwhelmed. Everyone knew that the task that lay ahead was going to require supernatural strength and divine intervention. They were no longer going to be able to count on me to do what I had always done. For the first time in my life, I was truly dependent on the people that walked slowly behind my wheelchair. I had become a burden to my loved ones, and I did not see any relief in sight. What did going home hold for me?

As part of the exit process, I had to show the nurses that I was able to walk out in the hallway for an extended stretch. I walked from my room down to the nurses' station. When I reached the station, I did a little victory dance. Everyone cheered as though I had walked on the moon. My father was crying and overcome with fear that I was going to hurt myself. His facial expression reminded me of how when I was 10, he would run behind my bicycle holding on to help me balance. It took me three times as long to learn because he was afraid to let me fall. But now, here I was walking on my own, wading in the water, after the storm. That short walk indicated that I was ready to go home. It also showed me what a long road ahead I had to walk.

> ***"...and the one less traveled has made all the difference" Robert Frost***

Visitors were still coming as we gathered my things in preparation to leave. Everyone was rejoicing over my return home. I was excited but very anxious. I knew that my family was anxious too; however, no one wanted to *rain* on my parade. My parents would return home to New York once I was safely in the house. We all knew, however, that although I was being released, I was still in the danger zone.

The nurses and doctors packaged me up and sent me home marked, ***"FRAGILE! HANDLE WITH CARE."*** Instructions, there were lots of instructions. "Don't wet the incisions! Don't lean on your elbows! Don't apply pressure to the chest area! Don't eat a lot of salt! Don't eat a lot of fat! Don't lift anything over 10 pounds! Don't walk up and down the stairs too often! Don't have marital relations!!!! Don't pick up your children! Don't drive the car! Don't return to work! Don't go back to complete graduate school! Don't miss your medication! **DON'T!.. .DON'T!...DON'T!...**

I was still in the danger zone, but I was wading in the water-HOMEWARD BOUND.

Chapter 18

A Table for Two

For where two or three gather in my name, there am I with them. Matthew 18:20 NIV

As the car pulled up to my front door my house was a sight for sore eyes. My ordeal had terrified me into thinking that I would never see this house again. But here I was home on January 26, 1999, just twelve days after my first heart attack.

Although the car was parked just a few yards from the door of the house, getting inside seemed like an impossible task. It took quite a while for me to unfold myself out of the car. The incisions in my chest hurt as I moved my upper body out of the car. The pain was excruciating, yet necessary for me to go inside the house. The incision in my leg hurt most of all. I had only used my legs minimally since the surgery and each step tore at the 18 inch gash, from where the vein had been removed. Pain radiated throughout my body as the morning painkillers were wearing off. In addition, it only took the slightest of efforts to induce shortness of breath and extreme exhaustion. Needless to say breathing was difficult during this task. Each step was more challenging than the previous, but I had to do it. Husband brought a folding chair out to the walkway of the house so that I could rest every few steps. Everyone present felt the pain as I walked towards my "new normal" life.

      Upon entering the house, everything felt familiar yet strange. It was reminiscent of having an experience of walking in a large parking lot and coming to a spot and saying, "I know I left my car parked right here," only to find it somewhere else. I approached the house saying, "I know I left my life parked right here," but I just could not seem to put my finger on it. It took quite a while for me to make it through the door. It was unbelievable that I was actually home. I had been thrust back into my world without the safety net of the hospital. There would not be any nurses, doctors, wheelchairs, breakfast carts, bed pans or I V bottles to rely on. No bells to ring or buttons to push; no team to call, just me, Husband and the Lord...and the ones that he would send.

My house was strangely quiet. J.C. and Sadie were gone. My precious new born baby and my precious two year old were with my in-laws because I was obviously in no condition to care for them. I was even too weak to care for myself. The separation anxiety was enormous and my broken heart needed mending. I knew that I would need to focus on recovery in order to ease the pain of being apart from my babies. It was a constant battle to quiet the raging thoughts in my head. Not only was I missing my babies, but I was missing out on their growth that was taking place minute by minute.

Children grow and change from day to day and I was missing the wonder of each new phase. I needed my baby in my arms, and I needed my big boy tugging at my shirt. I needed to touch their faces and hear them laugh. I needed to see the wonder in their eyes as they touched new things. I longed to lay them down in peace next to me and to hover over them with the love that comes from a mother. I wanted my whole family back. However, each time a melancholy thought came into my mind I focused on gratitude that although delayed, I was still alive to be a part of their precious lives.

Once inside the house, my family helped me to get to a chair in the kitchen. My Kitchen! My kitchen where just two weeks prior, I had packed my lunch with my famous homemade oatmeal, pecan cookies; sterilized bottles, packed baby bags; prepared meals, washed dishes and opened the refrigerator more times than I could recall. Now my kitchen was just an empty room. It had no life, only a table for two.

Tawanda Prince

　　Cooking has always been a pleasure for me, and on this day, I looked to my kitchen for comfort. After what seemed like forever, I gathered up enough strength to put together a meal. Yes, a meal. I was determined to find that "new normal" somewhere wedged between the "old normal" and today. I sat at the kitchen table and I used Husband as my extended arms and legs. He did not know how to cook but he was willing to assist me in whatever way that he could. He took some frozen chicken wings out of the freezer and sat them on the table in front of me. He gathered the casserole dish and the spices and I went to work. I seasoned the chicken and Husband put the dish in the oven. Next, I asked for a box of frozen spinach that could easily be prepared in the microwave oven. After that, I asked for a can of sweet potatoes so that I could prepare my favorite quick and easy candied yams on the stovetop. I was using the food to help bridge the gap between the old life and the new.

Shortly after my homecoming my parents had to return home to New York. I was not ready for them to go. It felt like that first day of college when parents drive off leaving their child standing on the sidewalk waving goodbye. The sense of abandonment pushed my emotions to another level. I did not want them to leave me; I needed them. We had been through birth, death and rebirth together, how could they leave me? They turned me over to Husband just as they had done six years prior, and it was painful. I saw in their eyes that they wanted to stay, but they had interrupted their lives since the beginning of my ordeal and it was time for them to return. Their departure left a big hole in my *heart*.

So there Husband and I sat at a table for two; just the two of us in this strange new world. Neither one of us able to express what we felt inside. Neither one of us aware of the road that lay ahead. Just the two of us, sitting at a table set for two that was missing two. J.C. and Sadie, the two that made our hearts complete were missing. Mom and Dad, the two that had been our rock were missing. Just the two who promised for better or worse; for richer or poorer; in sickness and in health; until parted by death. Just the two who had stumbled along for six years clinging to promises made and vows taken. Just the two with questions desperately seeking answers. Just the two wrapped up in a ball of confusion after the storm. Just the two grieving for days gone by. Just the two of us.

      We sat at that table for two, missing two, and ate dinner. Husband was relieved to have me there and we ate together as if for the first time. As we ate, my heart grew heavier by the minute. The thought of climbing the stairs to get to my bedroom was overwhelming. I knew that it was going to require strength that I had not yet ever tapped into. I also knew that once I reached the upper room, I would be there for an extended period of time, not able to return to a table for two for quite some time.

After dinner, I made the great effort to go upstairs. Husband helped me as much as he could but I had to reach way down into that reservoir of strength to make it to the top. It was a painful process. My chest was still very sore and fragile and my leg still felt the sensation of being ripped open. I knew that one wrong move would send me back to the hospital and possibly back to surgery. My heart beat faster and my breath grew shorter with each baby step. After what seemed like forever, I finally made it upstairs. It was clear that life at home was going to be far more challenging than hospital life had been.

Preparing for bed was also a slow process. Oddly enough, I was wearing part of what I was wearing when I went to the hospital with the the first heart attack. I recalled being dressed extra nice that day in my favorite outfit. It was a black, double breasted pants suit with a leopard collar. Oh the things that we get attached to. I was wearing the pants but Husband had brought me another blouse and had purchased a package of socks. My hair was a mess after the hospital ordeal, and I had not used my Mary Kay Cosmetics on my face in quite a while. As I stripped myself of my outerwear, I was not able to face the damage that had been done to my body.

The fear and anxiety mounted as Husband and I attempted to define a new routine. We quickly realized that our bedroom was not quite the same as the hospital room. Our bed was not able to adjust to accommodate my special needs. I was unable to lie flat and each position that I assumed increased the pain and discomfort. I could not apply any pressure to my elbows. I was uncomfortable on my side and of course lying on my stomach was out of the question. The only sense of relief that I could get was by reclining in a sitting position. Husband propped me up with pillows and I gently leaned back as far as possible. Needless to say it was very uncomfortable for both of us.

Sleep did not come easy that first night. Fear rushed in and stalked us, hovering like a ghost.

Tawanda Prince

Husband was restless and disturbed by the obvious changes in my breathing. In the still of the night, he could hear my irregular breathing pattern. As panic set in he shook me because he could hear long delays in the rhythms and he was afraid that THUNDER was knocking again. I was afraid too. Afraid of what? Afraid of dying I guess. There were no buttons to push so we had to rely on prayer to get us through the night. Morning was a long time coming and recovery would prove to be a long time coming also.

Chapter 19

After the Storm

Whatever you do, work at it with all your heart, as working for the Lord, not for human masters, since you know that you will receive an inheritance from the Lord as a reward. It is the Lord Christ you are serving. Colossians 3:23-24 NIV

It was painfully obvious that recovery was going to be an arduous task. It was no secret that the rug that had been snatched out from under me was torn into shreds. My heart and my life had been shattered into tiny pieces and reconstruction would require the Master's touch.

The Master, who had created the original vessel, knew the name and purpose of each broken piece. Only the Master could piece it back together and make it better. In the mirror, I looked like Tawanda, sounded like Tawanda and acted very much like Tawanda, but I was a broken vessel under construction. The storm had ravished me, thrashed me about and strewn me aside for dead, but God's master plan would not allow the storm to take me out.

The next morning reality fully set in. I was still aching from bandages vertically stretched joining my right side of my chest to my left. Various other bandages covered holes where tubes had once been. Blood caked up in crevices that remained unable to be washed. My movement was still greatly restricted. My head was heavy and my thoughts hazy from system overload. My strange body was in a familiar place that didn't look or feel the same. Husband forced me to look in the mirror at the scars. He stood with me as I surveyed he visual damage after the storm.

Oh how I longed for the ability to do even simple tasks that I had previously done. Things that I had previously taken for granted like taking a shower, holding my children, fixing breakfast, and even sleeping comfortably in my bed. I didn't think much about those things until I was unable to do them. I now had to incorporate a medicine regimen, new eating habits and a heart-healthy diet, modified activity levels and overall lifestyle adjustments.

    I watched Husband. He was completely overwhelmed by our circumstances and I could see the weight bearing down on him. I needed to lean on him, but I could tell the burden was much too heavy for his shoulders alone. We needed help and thank God help was on the way.

    When I was in the hospital my friend Marlene and her mom, Miss Bessie came to visit me. We had been friends and schoolmates growing up in the Bronx, New York and oddly enough, we had all reconnected after relocating to the area. Miss Bessie was concerned about my recovery at home. She knew the struggle that lay ahead in putting the pieces back together. Since Miss Bessie was retired, she devoted much of her time for volunteer efforts and graciously volunteered to visit daily and assist me with recovery, after the storm.

God truly answers prayers and supplies our every need. He works things out better than we could ever imagine. There was no way that we could have handled this period by ourselves. Both sets of grandparents were taking care of our children and Miss Bessie was on duty to take care of me.

She showed up bright and early that first morning after, ready to serve. She was an incredible blessing. Still unable to navigate the stairs, I remained in my room for several days. Miss Bessie became my feet and my hands, making sure that I wanted for nothing. She served with a heart of gladness and love, helping me to begin my "new normal" life.

Miss Bessie was there to make sure that each piece of the storm ravished vessel was put back together. Restoration is a process, and this process required patience and care. That is exactly what Miss Bessie rendered. She faithfully served to make the transition as smooth as possible. I had more questions than answers, and I had a long storm ravished road ahead of me. Miss Bessie helped me to focus on getting well and to keep my priorities in order. She did not allow anything or anybody to compromise my care, not even me.

I was weak in mind, body, soul and spirit and her presence was such a comfort to me. Day by day she ministered to me. She loved me as I took each painful step towards recovery. Her faithfulness in serving never wavered. She used her faith to help me to overcome. Miss Bessie believed in God's healing power and believed that I was going to make it through, even when it seemed impossible. Miss Bessie was a pillar of strength for me to lean on.

Days rolled into weeks, and weeks rolled into months and Miss Bessie continued to faithfully serve. Each day I grew stronger in my ability and in my faith. I rose each morning to face the challenge of reparation after the storm. Each day I could see things a little clearer as my soul was anchored in the Lord after being shipwrecked during the storm. There were many tears and many trials, but each morning I arose in triumph.

Eventually, my children returned from being with their grandparents and Miss Bessie helped me make the transition back to full time motherhood. I discovered during this time that every beat of my heart was tied to my children. I drew strength and courage from their love and need for me. I had to survive in order for them to thrive. Failure was not an option. God had given me life and was daily healing my broken heart. The scattered pieces from my shattered life were coming back together bit by precious bit, and each day that the sun rose and set was another demonstration of God's undying and unfailing love for me.

In the weeks and months to come, many people rose to the challenge of helping put the pieces back together of my shattered life. Neighbors, friends, family, co-workers and even strangers answered the tug at their heart strings to help a sister in need. I witnessed God do what seemed impossible through those that he sent my way. The outpouring of gifts, time and service were too numerable to name, but to each one who sowed a seed, my gratitude was overflowing.

Choose life. Choose life. Choose life. It was my daily challenge. Each day I had to make a choice to trust God fully, believe for healing of my "broken heart", and put in the work needed for recovery. I continued to grow stronger physically through a Cardiac Rehabilitation program, a modified diet and medication. My functionality and capacity improved with each step. I also put forth the effort for inner rehabilitation through counseling, pastoral care, reading God's Word and other inspirational books, healing conversations with friends and much love. After the storm, I took the time to discover, recover, celebrate, recreate and reinvent myself. I exercised my faith to restore that which had been shattered. Through this process I learned that no matter what storm comes my way, I must CHOOSE LIFE.

Chapter 20

Yet still I Rise

Therefore if any man be in Christ, he is a new creature: old things have passed away and behold all things have become new. 2 Corinthians 5:17 KJV

There has been so much water under the bridge since **THUNDER** knocked and the storm passed through. God has made me a new creature. Much like the creatures and sea monsters of the old horror films who emerged from the tempest. Nothing could keep them down. Neither weapons nor skilled seamen could destroy the sea monster. Just when it seemed they were pierced or wounded enough to die off, they would rise up out of the water more fierce than before.

Likewise God has made me a "SEE-monster." He has worked His powerful miracles in me for the entire world to "see". Just when it seemed that I was too wounded or devastated to rebound, God empowered me to rise from the tempest. I also arose from deep waters as a "SEE-monster" because I have greater vision and the capacity to SEE beyond what is in front of me, to the infinite possibilities. Not only did I rise up out of the deep, but I have emerged with more...MORE power, MORE faith, MORE trust, MORE boldness, MORE commitment, MORE conviction, MORE determination, MORE vision, MORE heart, MORE soul, MORE love, MORE peace, MORE "heartitude" and MORE like Him.

    Through the many things that have happened since January 1999, God has kept me. There were days when I could not see my way clear, yet God has kept me. My faith was challenged and stretched beyond anything I could ever imagine, yet God has kept me. God kept me through separation and divorce. God kept me through raising my children without a partner in my home. God has kept me through financial struggles which included near foreclosure on my house twice. God has kept me through broken heartedness and loneliness. God has kept me through rejection by friends, family and others. God kept me through managing my heart condition, for many years, without health insurance. God has kept me through faithfully carrying out my ministry although often rejected by the church. God has kept me through relocating to a new city. God has kept me through subsequent heart challenges including other surgeries, procedures and adjustments. Through it all God has kept me.

I can bear witness that when lightning strikes and **THUNDER** rolls, God provides for every need. When I was down to nothing, God was up to something. Every time that the darkness was about to overtake me, the light of the "Son" came shining through. God is a healer and His healing power has enabled me to rise above my condition and meet the challenges of each new day. Although my medical reports show that only 25% of my heart works, God equips me with what I need daily. God is my peace, and although the tempest may blow around me He gives me peace in the storm.

God is my shepherd who cares for me, feeds me, guides me, corrects me and comes after me when I get lost along the way. God has been my protector when the enemy has waged war against me and has been my banner which goes before me declaring victory. God has also been my strength equipping me with power, might and endurance. When **THUNDER** knocked and shattered my heart, God loving put each piece back together again.

    Since **THUNDER** knocked at my heart, I am living my life with "heartitude." That is, living with boldness in passionate pursuit of what God wants for my life. Simply put, "heartititude" is faith in action. I have had many challenges and made lots of mistakes, but I can truly say I am living the good life. The good life is not a perfect life but is all GOOD because it is all GOD.

Chapter 21

The Test of the Storm

The Lord spoke to Job out of the storm. Job 40:6 NIV

The good thing about a storm is that eventually it passes over. No storm lasts forever, but the effects often do. Although everyone's storm is different, there are some common elements that come with every storm.

With every storm there are warning signs. Often times we depend on the weather scientists and meteorologists to tell us of storm potential. The atmospheric conditions predict that a storm is on the horizon. Many times we are even warned of the severity and duration of the storm. The storms are rated based on expected intensity of storm activity. Physical evidence usually matches the storm predictions. We can feel a shift in the atmosphere. Clouds begin to move in and the winds begin to change. Darkness and gray replace sunshine and blue. There is often a change in climate and the environment grows cold. Our senses become attuned to the atmospheric change, and we watch and we wait in anticipation of the ensuing storm.

So it is with the storms of life. Situations often foretell that a storm is at hand. Oftentimes, there is visible evidence that a storm is imminent. In your spirit one can begin to feel a change in the atmosphere. Clouds move in and the winds of trouble begin to blow. Darkness and gray replace sunshine and blue. A spirit of heaviness invades your peace and the climate begins to grow cold.

Despite the weatherman's warnings and predictions, there are some who do not heed or recognize when a storm is at hand. They fail to respond appropriately by preparing for what lies ahead. Some are so caught up with other things that they miss the predictions and warning signs. Far in the distance, **THUNDER** is knocking, but they don't heed.

Likewise with the storms of life, people fail to acknowledge or heed the warnings. Some people even set up conditions that are conducive to a storm. Furthermore, there are those who acknowledge the warnings but remain unprepared. Although they know the potential for tumultuous activity, they continue along. As **THUNDER** knocks far off in the distance, they don't heed.

With nature, as the storm moves in closer, the atmosphere begins to change drastically. Dark clouds hover down low, casting a shadow on everything. Wind gusts pick up and blow around things that are not securely anchored. Thunder roars louder and lightening is often visible. Everything in the environment is disturbed. Many run for shelter and sometimes relocate due to imminent danger from the storm. Rains descend and water rises, making travel difficult. Trees blow, with each limb bowing to the power of the storm. Man becomes so small up against the greatness of the storm. Although we are knowledgeable about the conditions, we are limited in our effort to protect ourselves. We must rely on the mercy and grace of **THUNDER**.

We find ourselves in the same position when the storms of life move in. The atmosphere begins to change drastically. Things grow dark as the winds of trouble blow. We feel darkness pressing in on every side. We are often tossed about as the storm rages. The winds of trouble and adversity blow around and displace anyone who is not anchored in the **TRUTH**. ***Jesus saith unto him, I am the way, the truth, and the life: no man cometh unto the Father, but by me." John 14:6 KJV*** Any tree that is not rooted deeply enough will blow over. So it is with us.

There are different types of storms. There are tropical storms, hurricanes, tornados, typhoons and tsunamis. Although each of these falls under the category of "storm," they vary drastically in power and effect. Some of these cause a little discomfort and inconvenience; some cause major devastation.

Nevertheless, they all bring about change in the environment. Many times things are never the same after a storm.

When the storms of life hit us, they too come in varying degrees of intensity. Some cause a little discomfort and inconvenience, and some cause major devastation, leading to transformation. It is no secret that storms bring change. That change usually affects an area of our lives that would not transform otherwise. In order for God to get our full attention and yielded spirits, we must go through a storm or tsunami, whichever will yield God's desired results.

Once a storm passes over, the time comes to assess the damage, evaluate the change, and count the cost. Just after the storm, there is an eeriness that pervades as people emerge out of hiding. People begin to look for the effects. Fallen trees, broken limbs, debris, shattered windows, floods and power outages are visible effects of the storm. Oftentimes there are things that are not as obvious, such as water damage in the foundations of buildings, leaks, elements in nature, cleansing, mold and mildew. It takes time to discover these things. At first glance, these things masquerade as normal but in time, the discord, destruction, and disease makes itself known. What was once so right is suddenly so wrong.

No matter what the damages may be, repairs are necessary. Sometimes repairs take years. First one must clear away the debris and fallout. Oh how it can scatter about sometimes, seeping into the most unlikely places. Following multiple paths that take time to trace and recover. Days…weeks…months…and sometimes years pass by and one will discover a broken piece of debris. Each piece is a reminder of the power of **"THUNDER."**

So it is with our lives, there is fallout from our storms. Pieces of our lives are shattered and scattered about. Debris and fallout litter our spirits and hinder our recovery efforts. We too experience temporary power outages that leave us in the dark and depleted.

Things fall apart, and we struggle to piece them back together. We often require help from others to assist the "clean up" effort. Sometimes we are so devastated by the storm that we are unable to do it ourselves. In fact we often cannot even envision wholeness and struggle to believe that restoration is even possible. Some are even so paralyzed after the storm that they just stop and wonder why.

    Repairs and recovery can be a lengthy and tedious process. Like in the aftermath of Hurricane Katrina, ongoing effort didn't seem to make even a small dent in the recovery tasks. Each step seemed to unmask even more wreckage from the storm. Lost lives, homes, businesses and services were immeasurable. Many losses will even remain unidentified for years to come and perhaps forever. Clean up efforts were overshadowed by the reality that for those who survived the storm, life will never be the same.

    Our personal storms are often the same. It takes a team effort to initialize repairs and recovery. A team of doctors, family, neighbors and friends, other professionals and clergy compile efforts to heal the broken pieces. Sometimes the damage from the storm is so severe that these efforts seem futile. But by and by, the warmth of the "Son" begins to shine through, casting a gleam of hope in the midst of devastation. The team's efforts are multiplied by the power and presence of God after the storm. It is then keenly evident that God was there in the storm and all is not lost.

When lightning strikes and thunder rolls, we must hold fast to the truth that storms produce fertile ground. The rain soaks deep beneath the surface stimulating germination, which leads to growth. To the naked eye, what appears to be devastation is really transformation. Though it may appear to be a wipe out, it is in fact a chance for a fresh start. Once the clean-up effort is underway, signs of new life appear. The new is often better than the old.

When we take the hit from our personal storms, it is the beginning of our transformation. Our growth would otherwise be stunted without the storm experience. Sometimes the seeds of change will not grow without the flood of adversity. At first, it is difficult to see the possibilities, but bit-by-bit, the transformation takes place. Sometimes it is difficult to count the cost of the damage. However, once growth takes place, it is impossible to count the blessing of transformation. We must remember that God wants to use the storm to bless us. Storms are necessary for growth; and growth is necessary for purpose. Though the storms may rage through our lives, ***"All things work together for good for those who are the called according to his purpose." Romans 8:28 KJV***

After the storm, we become keenly aware that God's grace is sufficient. Also, His will can never lead us where His grace cannot keep us. The purpose of every storm is to move us toward our purpose. It becomes easier to recover when we grab hold of the truth that it is not about us. Because "all things" are working together, my storm for instance is merely a cog in the wheel of purpose.

Another blessing in recovery is discovery. The definition of discover is to uncover, disclose and expose. It is after the devastation that we "discover" who we really are, who God is and who our co-laborers are. We discover that we have supernatural strength, faith and endurance. We are able to stand after the destruction and "bend our knees," to begin to pick up the pieces. When we "bend our knees" we assume the position of prayer, humility and worship.

Every knee should bow and every tongue should confess that Jesus Christ is Lord. Philippians 2:10 KJV

We also, discover that God has fortified us and equipped us to handle the transformation brought by the storm. We discover that we are more than conquerors. Just as "the whole is equal to the sum of its parts," we are the sum of our storms. Each little storm has prepared us for when **THUNDER** really knocks.

Moreover, we discover the awesomeness of God. We learn that God is greater than the sum of our storms. We learn that God is God all by Himself. He has the "GREAT" plan, power and provision for our storms. Nothing takes Him by surprise. We may not have foreseen the storms but God in His infinite wisdom not only foresees the storm but He predestines the glory, which is the result of the storm.

For whom He foreknew, He predestined…moreover whom He predestined, these He also called; whom He called He also justified and whom He justified these He also glorified. Romans 8:29-30 NKJV.

What is so wonderful is that God only allows the storms for those whom He has chosen. Furthermore, God only calls us because He knows that He can trust us with "the call." The truth is that all things really do work together for good for those who are the called according to His purpose, not just your desire. The storm is necessary for His purpose.

Because God is a God of restoration, His glory is shown marvelously in the recovery and discovery after the storm. In fact, God specializes in creating something out of nothing. His very essence is to bring life and resurrection after death and destruction. Jesus' death, burial and resurrection are the blueprint for our storm experiences. God is true to His word, but He requires our faith, trust and work. Faith without works is dead. His glory is made manifest as we work toward restoration after the storm.

Thirdly, we dis-cover who our co-laborers are. It is always surprising who is left standing with you amongst the rubble. Amazingly it is rarely the people who you thought would be there. You discover that God often sends "storm chasers." These are the ones who just show up, to help us go up. They are there to lend spiritual, physical, emotional and financial assistance to help us put the pieces back together again. Sometimes, we even overlook these helpers because our eyes and hearts are fixed on those whom we thought would help us repair and recover. It is not until we set our eyes on God the author and finisher of our faith and on the ones that He sends to us that we can effectively move into recovery.

Those co-laborers are sometimes unaware of the pivotal role that they play in God's plan and purpose. These people are simply obedient to the tug at their spirits to spring into action. Sometimes God will use them to do something great in your life and sometimes it will be something so small that you could easily overlook it. Be careful not to disregard the help that comes, even if it comes from the most unlikely source.

We must also be aware that these storm chasers have seasons. Only some will be with us for the long haul. We will establish a deep connection, jointly fitting together like two pieces in a puzzle. However, there are those who will only be with us for just a minute. Their contribution to recovery will be quick and may even appear to be insignificant. But we must resist the temptation to dismiss their efforts. Also, we must refrain from being angry about those brief encounters and about those who let you down. Remember, that everything is carefully orchestrated by God, to work out for our good.

The funny thing about storms is that if we make it to the other side we are bound to play a key role in helping someone else to get over their storm. God recycles the devastation of our storms to bring new life to someone else. It is a part of the circle of life. Furthermore, God requires those of us who have recovered to not only help others, but to tell others of His goodness. The Word says,

They overcome him by the blood of the lamb and by the word of their testimony... Rev 12:11 KJV

That means the shedding of the blood of the lamb is connected to our testimony, the two go hand in hand. In this, God will always get the glory if we remember to connect the two, blood and testimony.

It is nobody's business how God chooses survivors. No one really knows or understands the "why's," but we do know that those who He has chosen, through it all He justified and glorified them. Not for their own good pleasure but for His. Furthermore, when the Master has need of a vessel, although broken by the wind and rain, He has the power to make it over again.

Ultimately, these life storms tell us who God is, who we are, and apart from Him, we are nothing. These storms give us the opportunity to come out of our skin and emerge as a vessel of honor; fit for use by the King of Kings and Lord of Lords. This refinement is not of our doing but in fact perfected as a result of the storm.

Amazingly, in our "newness" we often forget the true agony and devastation suffered through the storm. We simply cling to the cross and bask in the glory of the "Son".

Author's Note

Reference from Page 104

If you declare with your mouth, "Jesus is Lord," and believe in your heart that God raised Him from the dead, you will be saved. For it is with your heart that you believe and are justified, and it is with your mouth that you profess your faith and are saved. As Scripture says, "Anyone who believes in Him will never be put to shame." For there is no difference between Jew and Gentile, the same Lord is Lord of all and richly blesses all who call on him, for, "Everyone who calls on the name of the Lord will be saved." Romans 10:9-13 NIV

God wants to save you and receive you as his own, but you must first receive him. If you desire to allow the blood of Jesus to cleanse you from all sin and unrighteousness pray the following prayer out loud:

Tawanda Prince

Dear Lord,

I confess that I am a sinner. I believe that Jesus Christ died on the cross of Calvary for my sins. I believe that you raised Him from the dead and that His resurrection took away my sin. I believe that there is power in the blood of Jesus and that I am saved. Draw near unto me oh Lord that I may know you. I repent of my sins and wrong doing. Help me to live as a child of God redeemed by the blood of the lamb that was slain. Thank you Jesus for coming into my life and saving me.

If you just prayed this prayer, you have chosen life. God desires to have a relationship with you now that you belong to him. You must build a relationship with God just like you do with all of those that you love. Spending quiet time with God reading His Word and praying will draw you closer. Also, find a church that teaches the Word of God from the Holy Bible that will help you to grow in the area of Christian living.

It is important to note that even when you are saved, there will be storms. I would even dare say that especially because you are saved there will be storms in your life. But you now have the blessed assurance that there is power in **the blood** even in the midst of the storm.

And we know that in all things, God works for the good of those who love Him, who have been called according to His purpose. For those God foreknew He also predestined to be conformed to the likeness of His Son, that he might be the firstborn among many brothers. And those He predestined, He also called, those He called, He also justified; those He justified, He also glorified. Romans 8: 28-30 NIV

Tawanda Prince

Thunder Knocking at my Heart

Made in the USA
Charleston, SC
29 July 2016